Praise for *Feast*

"*Feast* is a beautiful, heartbreaking, and life-affirming story that anyone who has ever struggled to define a healthy relationship with food will be able to relate to. I couldn't put it down."

—Nicola Kraus, coauthor of *The Nanny Diaries*

"Heartfelt, heartbreaking, and courageously generous, *Feast* is one of the most memorable and important debuts I've ever read. With beautiful lyricism and unflinching storytelling, Hannah Howard weaves together addiction, love, fear, sexism, insecurity, ambition, and trauma in a way I've never seen done before. As with everything, with every life, *Feast* isn't a story about one thing, but rather how intersecting, manifold, and even contradictory things make up a life. It's a story about the miraculousness of becoming yourself. A must-read for anyone who's ever wanted to escape their body, for anyone who has loved deeply and wrongly, for anyone who has dared to forgive themselves."

—Morgan Parker, author of *There Are More Beautiful Things Than Beyoncé*

"Brave and beautifully written, *Feast* is an addictive read. Hannah Howard brilliantly captures the complicated relationships so many of us have with food, love, sex, and ourselves in lyrical prose that will make you hungry for more."

—Kimberly Rae Miller, author of *Beautiful Bodies*

"Hannah Howard's memoir, *Feast*, is a courageous exploration of vulnerability, desire, and addiction, set to the thrilling backdrop of New York City's nascent foodie culture. It's a must-read for food lovers and makers alike."

—Tia Keenan, author of *The Art of the Cheese Plate: Pairings, Recipes, Style, Attitude*

"Word for word, sentence for sentence, and chapter for chapter, Hannah Howard has written a hard-to-put-down book—one that is heart-wrenching and, ultimately, uplifting and inspirational."

—David Farley, author of *An Irreverent Curiosity*

"In her revealing new memoir, Hannah Howard tells a raw tale of her love-hate relationship with eating, delving into the dark side of our food-obsessed culture. Between tormented relationships with chefs, a moth-to-a-flame attraction to the food industry, and her own struggles with an eating disorder, Howard emerges stronger and wiser, encouraging readers that yes, it can get better."

—Gabriella Gershenson, food writer and editor

"An immensely entertaining debut by a writer whose precision and self-preservation are that of a jet-fighter pilot—incisive, totally aware of the forces around her and her own fallibility."

—Steven Jenkins, author of *Cheese Primer*

FEAST

FEAST

True Love

IN AND OUT OF THE KITCHEN

HANNAH HOWARD

Published by Little A, New York

www.apub.com

Amazon, the Amazon logo, and Little A are trademarks of Amazon.com, Inc., or its affiliates.

ISBN-13: 9781503942578 (hardcover)
ISBN-10: 1503942570 (hardcover)
ISBN-13: 9781503942585 (paperback)
ISBN-10: 1503942589 (paperback)

Cover design by Faceout Studio

Printed in the United States of America

First edition

To the cooks, bakers, cheesemakers, servers, grocers, and bartenders who love food and who struggle.

Tonight when you are ripped open
down to the very seed,
when you feel that hunger, know:
you are not what you pack up now for next year,
you will not be put up on the shelf in jars.

—*Rena Mosteirin, "Milkweed Coat"*

Contents

Cookies

On the night of my last binge, New York City is raw. Even my teeth twinge with cold. It's November, I'm twenty-four years old, and I have just moved back to Manhattan after a stint managing a fine dining restaurant in Philadelphia. I feel at home for the first time in years. Everyone is welcome here, everything allowed. On my worst days, now, I feel pregnant with loneliness, exhausted from loathing my body and the rest of me; I walk east on 95th Street to the park and think, *I live here*, which is sweet consolation. New York buoys me up and up again. I rarely miss my boyfriend Ari—ex-boyfriend now—although I feel guilty for abandoning him in Philadelphia. He calls me most nights, late. I always regret when I answer.

After looking at dozens of tiny but inordinately expensive NYC apartments—maybe the kitchen consists of one burner and a mini-fridge; or the bedroom is actually a living room, which the landlord needs to walk through to access her own bedroom—I find a little slice of the Upper West Side which is actually kind of (not quite, but I'll take *kind of*) affordable. I sign the lease on the spot.

I love my new studio on West 95th Street, how the light saunters in every morning, the wide countertop that separates the kitchen from my new post-Ari mattress in its wrought iron frame, the window ledges that I use as bookshelves. Mostly I love that it's mine.

I hang a sparkly red tapestry I bought with my best friend Ursula in Thailand. The quilt on my bed is bright as watermelon. If I lean to the left and squint just so, I can catch the start of the green expanse of Central Park outside my window, past avenues of traffic and scarf-wearing ladies wheeling shopping carts.

My parents invite me to dinner at their friends' Upper East Side apartment. I walk across Central Park in new motorcycle boots, filled with a particular New York brand of hope. Everyone here is fulfilling vast dreams to make billions, redefine modern dance, launch artisanal ginger ale companies, and they are all in the park tonight: crowds, dogs, tourists, families, the setting sun and its reflection against the still surface of the reservoir, the last few burnt-orange leaves illuminating the trees.

At Joy and Alec's place, intricate carpets overlap each other. A gray puppy jumps its little legs onto my knees. Joy pours me a glass of wine in a glass as big as their puppy. Alec shakes my hand before pulling me into a hug.

"Your mom tells me you have a new job. Fairway, huh?" I'm tall, but Alec towers over me benevolently. He speaks with the slightest Greek accent.

"That's right."

"I can't get enough of their smoked salmon."

"We're Fairway smoked salmon addicts," Joy agrees. "And the mini bagels, the mini everything bagels! Come eat. We're going to sit in the living room like the slobs we are."

But nothing feels slobbish about this endeavor. Their sofas are upholstered in silk and the giant coffee table is set with porcelain chopsticks and goblets for water. Dissonant jazz plays on the speakers. I wonder if this is how everyone lives on the Upper East Side.

"Did you get a haircut?" my dad asks. "I like your hair."

He is trying to be nice; my hair is the same as always. "No haircut. But thanks."

"Well." Joy gestures to the spread of sushi rolls and slivers of sashimi, gyoza and edamame, little bowls of ginger and wasabi. The feast covers the entire table. "Don't be shy."

My dad fills his plate first. My mom pulls a soybean from its green shell with her teeth. At first, I partake like a normal human being, dip a salmon avocado roll in soy sauce, add a dab of wasabi. And then another and another. Everyone is eating; a pause in the conversation.

Then, there's a shift. Something is awakened in me, a hunger that feels like a foreign, malicious force curled up in my stomach and reaching its monster limbs into my mouth and through my hands. I can't stop eating. My mom gives me a sideways glare. I know that look, the same one from when I was a kid. It means *You are eating a lot and I am noticing and it is not okay.* It means *You are not a skinny girl and you are not okay.* The only thing worse is when she actually says, out loud, "You know, dinner is coming." Or "Save some for everyone else." Or "Don't you think you've had enough to eat, maybe?"

I wait for my mom to say one of those things, or something worse, but she turns to Joy.

"How is your aunt? Oh, I'm forgetting her name."

"June is healthy as a horse, with killer lipstick. We just celebrated her ninety-fourth birthday."

Mom turns away from Joy to give me The Look again. I see what I usually see in her eyes—embarrassment, judgment. And past all that, I see something new. Compassion?

I am practically snuggled up with Mom and Dad on Alec and Joy's sofa, but the conversation feels far away. I can't stop hand to mouth to hand to mouth, no matter how much I will myself and no matter how much I hate myself for my lack of self-control, my irrepressible gluttony. I hate the bulk of my body, and I hate that I am failing to shrink it. I watch the way my thighs squish and unfurl onto the sofa.

Somehow I manage to stop eating sushi before the entire tray is consumed. Joy and Alec's fluffy dog curls up in my lap, its little head rests, soft on my knee.

"So tell us about Fairway. Do you know the secret of the smoked salmon yet?" Joy asks.

"I only know the secrets of the cheese. I'm starting behind the cheese counter. It's a temporary situation until they figure out a job in the office for me. But the cheese is right next to the deli counter, where we have all the lox and the geniuses who slice it."

Joy and Alec's kindness feels as soft as the pup, and I find it touching that they want to know about the minutiae of my life. I tell them about the light in the morning in my new apartment, Central Park out the window. I tell them about Fairway, the way I spent my first day breaking down a wheel of Parmigiano-Reggiano, how we use the rinds to flavor soup.

Then dessert is served: a giant plate of cookies, set right in front of me.

"They're just from the deli next door, but I think they're the most outrageous cookies in New York," Alec says, proud of the cookies.

"We're not really sweets people," my dad chimes in. He must be using the royal we; cookies are my favorite.

"We really shouldn't be eating them either," Joy says.

My mom looks at me again. I don't meet her eyes.

There are five of us at the table and probably enough cookies for a party of twenty, or even more. Chocolate chip, oatmeal raisin, butterscotch, peanut butter. The cookies are fat, round, as big as my face. Everything else fades out of focus. All I see are cookies.

I am Odysseus and the cookies are sugar sirens.

My parents and their friends fade to a fuzzy scrim.

I start with a little wedge each of oatmeal raisin and chocolate chip. That seems a reasonable way to start. But it also seems reasonable that I should try the other varieties, because they indeed turn out to be exemplary cookies—sweet but not too sweet, crunchy but with give, buttery and dense. The cookie sends a rush, electric almost, from my mouth to my brain. The other cookies, from which I snap off pieces to chew on slowly, are excellent, too. And by this point, I haven't eaten a whole cookie, just pieces, which doesn't feel like enough, really, so I eat some more pieces, and then some more. It's a crime to leave a piece of cookie, broken, naked like that, prone on the platter. It's my duty to eat it. The rush vibrates and surges to my stomach, my temples. My fat thighs disappear from underneath me. I feel the sugar and the butter surge to my toes, as if I have been switched on. I transform.

My mom's eyes say *cease and desist*, but more cookies are the only answer to the problem of her embarrassment, and of my own. I willfully lose track of how many cookies I eat. Eight? Twelve? More?

The gigantic platter is empty, save for some crumbs. It takes all my energy, not diving into those crumbs. Still, we laugh and sip our wine like nothing is awry, and the dog sits at my feet now, panting, until it's time to go home. Everyone hugs me goodbye like I am human, not a cookie monster.

They are wrong. I am all monster, wired, ravenous, manic. I get a cab home because I can't fathom the interminable wait for the subway or the long walk with myself across Central Park. My face is hot with humiliation.

At my building, I ride the elevator to the eleventh floor. Inside, I don't take off my shoes. I don't take off my coat. I go straight to the fridge and empty its contents: leftover pasta, bag of grapes (I leave the garlic cloves, salad greens, milk). I eat the pasta and the grapes so fast I hardly register them. The pasta is lubed up with olive oil, and it glides down my throat. The grapes I inhale by the handful, their skins snapping around juicy flesh.

I don't keep a whole lot of food in my kitchen for fear of exactly this. Sometimes I manage to go for a week without a binge, a month, even two, but other times I am ravaging my kitchen every night in insatiable panic. In my cabinet: a bag of dark chocolate chips, a box of cereal (the super-healthy kind, but that doesn't matter when you devour a whole box in one sitting), some dried figs, a half-eaten jar of almond butter. I lay out the goods on my countertop. I will eat every last bit. Waves of nausea pummel me, but I keep going. Heaping spoonfuls of the almond butter, then I scrape out the sides of the jar until my knife scratches empty plastic. The almond goo is glue on my tongue, the back of my mouth, the insides of my stomach. I need to scarf every last bit. I tilt the bag that lines the cereal box down my throat, sucking up the cereal pulp. The figs instantly make me want to puke, the seeds stick in my teeth, but I eat every one, barely pausing to chew. The chocolate chips—they're the good stuff. I manage to save them for last.

When everything is gone I open the fridge again, and then the cabinet, looking for more food. I am desperate. There's some raw quinoa, a softening apple I need to toss. The food quiets my panic. Without it, dread rises in my chest, my heart beats gunfire.

I think of going downstairs, out into the night. The fro-yo place is still open. I could get a bucket-sized vanilla yogurt smothered in all the candy and sprinkles and chocolate sauce. I could go to the grocery store and restock my reserves with cereal and chocolate and maybe some more cookies. Cookies for twenty people aren't enough for me. Not even close. I am possessed.

Somehow I manage to kick off my shoes. They ricochet across the floor.

I use the food because it works. It is an instant cure to whatever ails me, save the paltry price of the morning after—waking up and needing to barf and not being able to, vowing to eat nothing for a day, a week; the self-imposed, relentless suffering. When my friend Amanda didn't invite me to her sixth-grade sleepover, when my thighs rubbed together under my blue polyester school uniform, when I listened to easy conversation from the solitary confines of my college dorm room and felt loneliness drowning me, food was my friend. And when I won a poetry prize, and the sun shone on a springy day, and my chest swelled with love, with lust, there food was, an ever-loyal companion. Sure, food is my answer to anxiety, sadness, boredom, anger, but also to excitement, possibility, and joy.

And just like starving is the answer, bingeing is the answer.

Life is big and scary. Food is constant, safe, dependable.

Food blots everything out and calms everything down, draws the shades and tucks me in. Cozy. Miserable. Numb.

After devouring the cookies and the complete contents of my kitchen, I am still anxious and lonely. Neither the cookies, the pasta, nor the chocolate have ameliorated the constant tape that plays in my head. Often, postbinge, I feel a sweet relief, a stillness. Instead, tonight, my brain taunts me: *You fat piece of shit.* I miss Ari. My new life and new job, my new apartment in New York City, they are all supposed to be a new beginning, a fresh start, and I have ruined it by stuffing myself past the limits of what is bearable. The new me is supposed to be the thinnest me.

The physical evidence of my binge is clear: I am sweaty and distended, flooded with nausea, sore and shaky. My skin hurts, like it may burst around my expanding stomach, where I can clearly feel my pulse. But it's worse in my head, as if my brain is turning to silky puree in a food processor. Relief never comes.

My trusty companion has let me down. All that food has done nothing to quiet my demons. I cannot escape myself.

I throw my coat off my shoulders and onto the floor. In bed, my head crackles with radio static. I think I might throw up but I don't throw up. I rarely throw up, postbinge. Tonight I push two, three fingers down my throat, really try hard, but my reflexes are stubborn. The food stays, as usual. I feel it gumming up my insides.

I marinate my sheets in hot sweat. I don't sleep.

Peking Duck

Behind the stained-glass windows of my childhood home in Baltimore, there is surely something good cooking: cauliflower, crunchy with cumin seeds, or a big pot of chicken stew.

My mom works hard all day, but, on the corner of Calvert and 27th Street, she makes us dinner nearly every night. I set the table, my dad washes the dishes, and the chicken marsala, garlicky shrimp, cod over smoky chickpeas, turkey sausages with sweet red peppers, haddock coated with panko and panfried 'til crispy—those meals that made the kitchen steamy and the house fragrant—are the delicious fruits of my mom's effort. "It's my therapy," she says, chopping an onion and throwing it in sizzling oil. Sometimes she lets me help.

"Will you peel the shrimp?" She hates peeling the crustaceans, says it irritates her skin. I love slithering the cold bodies out of their plasticky shells. I peel. We sing along to Bonnie Raitt.

Food lights me up, the buttercup skin of squash blossoms, the yeasty warmth of bread. There is no better place than the kitchen. In Mom's kitchen, I feel lucky.

Weekdays are blue polyester uniform jumpers and basketball practice and elaborate playground games. And Saturdays, Saturdays are big days. My mom and I bid my dad adieu and off we go on a magical, mystical grocery-procuring adventure. It is coveted time with my mom, who is always busy with a stressful job and a noisy beeper.

First we stop at the sunny farmers market in my neighborhood, Charles Village. We take a small walk up the sidewalk, concrete shimmery with glass shards, and suddenly the streets are full of vendors selling jams and jellies, bright cherries and summertime peaches, baskets of arugula and lush, leafy things, stalks of asparagus in spring, shiny eggplants, and elephantine zucchini. There are dreadlocked musicians playing guitars, shaking tambourines, singing. It's hot and bright and Baltimore winks at me. We share a secret, my city and me.

My tummy is rumbling, and my mind is on breakfast. Maybe it's an elephant's ear from the impossibly elegant Parisian woman who presides over a table of croissants, éclairs, and madeleines. The palmier is the size of my face. I would hold it in two hands, anticipating the joy in its flaky, buttery goodness.

Or should I go savory? The mushroom lady's oyster mushrooms, enokis, and hens-of-the-woods look like a forest. She sets up a grill on which she sears meaty portobellos and warms up fresh pitas. Plumes of 'shroom smoke fill the morning sky. The pitas get stuffed with the hot mushrooms, a handful of milky feta, greens, and a dousing of hot sauce. This is an awesome breakfast. I watch my mom's joy at her own mushroom sandwich. It makes mine taste even better.

Next is the Near East Bakery. I am a kid in a candy shop. The candy: bins of pistachios, juicy figs, massive blocks of halvah, and barrels upon barrels of shiny olives. The olives are my dad's favorite, especially the fat, wrinkly black ones. He eats them with his fingers, spitting out the pits. I am proud to like them, too.

Egyptian soap operas play on a little TV by the registers, women in black eyeliner palm their foreheads in black and white as my mom and I load up on grape leaves, fragrant spices, and doughy breads stuffed with fava beans and sprinkled with za'atar.

Next up, Mastellone's, where we watch Mrs. Mastellone make mozzarella behind the counter, her arms swinging as she pulls and pulls and molds the curds. She sometimes offers me a piece of the just-made, still-warm mozz. It tastes so milky rich I feel shock waves, feel almost too lucky. My mom gathers fresh lasagna noodles, gold-green olive oil, San Marzano tomatoes, sausages, and big bunches of basil. Me, I'm still watching Mrs. Mastellone's pendulous arms, the weeping cheese. I am rapt.

My mom will cook our bounty into meals for the week. Even when she's drained from work, she will chop garlic at home at 6:30, 7:00. She will boil water for pasta, brown sage-scented turkey sausage on the stove, filling our home with something beyond just dinner.

In the school cafeteria amid a sea full of PB&Js and ham and cheese on white bread, I dig into my fava bean pie. Sometimes I am embarrassed, but today I am satisfied by starch and spice, excited. My meal satisfies my stomach and something deeper. On my best days, I don't want to be like everyone else.

I am not a cool girl. I always have friends, wonderful friends, and yet my identity as an outsider feels fixed from as far back as I can remember. Since plowing through the *Little House on the Prairie* books once and then immediately again.

The cool girls are the cute girls, tiny, compact. I am the tallest, towering, ungainly. The only Jew in my class, and then one of only two. In a sea of blondes, my hair is nearly black. I am a city girl among suburban princesses.

But most importantly, I am not thin enough.

This sums it all up. This is my curse, my refrain, true as my name.

In dance class, we are surrounded by 360 degrees of mirrors. They are sort of cheap, so that if you pirouette into them, they wobble, and your reflection quivers. I stand in the back row, always, my head poking out, ruining the neat hedge of my classmates' blonde heads. I look anywhere but the mirrors, fixing my gaze on the scuffed flooring. My toes, I think, are not so hideous. When my eyes meet my own face, my body, I fantasize about lopping off whole parts: the flesh of my preteen thighs, inches of height.

The cool girls don't worry about weight, or so I imagine. They are effortlessly, magically skinny. My middle school classmate Astor, a burgeoning soap opera star, can be found eating French fries by the trayful during lunch. She is long and lean and slim as that cafeteria fry. Is she throwing up in the yellow, airless bathroom after lunch? Rumor says so, but I never see it. "People are just jealous," my friend Steph says.

In fifth grade, we take a girls' road trip. We pile into my mom's Honda: me, Mom, Mom's friend from college, my Steph. We are driving to the Delaware shore. It is fall and the air is electric with chill. We stop for coffees for the grown-ups, hot chocolates for us with white clouds of whipped cream on top.

"The whipped cream is the best part," I say. I could dive into a whipped cream ocean.

"It's totally the best," Steph agrees. "The hot chocolate doesn't even matter."

"We should reverse the ratio and have big cups of whipped cream, with a little hot chocolate for garnish." My mom and her friend are no longer listening to us.

"We should open a whipped cream café," says Steph. I already thought she was a genius, but now I am sure.

At the café checkout, I ask my mom to buy a bag of gummy worms. I never ask for candy; we never eat candy at home, ever, but this feels like a special occasion and the fluorescent worms call to me through their cellophane. I am surprised when she says yes.

In the car, I open the crinkly package, offer the gummies to my mom, her friend, Steph. Nobody wants one, and so I set out to eat the whole bag.

"You're going to be sick," Mom warns, but I am not deterred.

"I don't think I will."

I am right, I don't get sick.

"Wow," Mom's friend says, herself overweight. "It's amazing that you can eat like that without consequences."

Without consequences!

Our fifth-grade class hosts a period party to celebrate our forthcoming womanhood. There is cake, red with food dye for symbolism. Moms sit in folding chairs at the front of the classroom and take turns telling us about the first time they found a smudge in their underwear. "People used to call it 'the curse,'" Steph's mom says. "But we are lucky to be women." We listen. My mom works hard, so she rarely frequents the mom-filled parent events at my school. She offers to come anyway, sometimes, but I like that school is my autonomous territory so I refuse. Still, she tells me about finding blood in her panties, how her grandmother slapped her across the face, as was custom. Nobody slaps me. I am second in the class to get my period. I tell everyone. I am proud, a trendsetter.

The boobs come next, and fast. I am less excited about them. When I run in gym class, in basketball practice, they tug at me. They are in the way. They make me take up more space, and taking up space is the worst curse. I blame them for feeling perpetually bulky and thundering. I feel like a cartoonish matron with a mountain range of a bosom. I long for cuteness. I am twelve.

At a sleepover at Steph's, she taps me on the shoulder. "Um, you made a small mess in the bathroom. Can you clean it up?"

I don't see it until she points it out to me—a smudge of brownish red on the lip of the toilet. She hands me a paper towel. Her freckles are buried in her blushing. It's now that I understand the curse.

With the start of middle school, our uniform switches from bright-blue polyester jumpers to bright-blue polyester skirts. The material is the same—so stiff and synthetic we think it won't burn in a fire, won't so much as melt. I picture our uniform skirt, proud, brilliant cobalt in a smoldering mess of gray debris. But the skirts can be rolled up at the waist, and let down for Ms. Johnson's reproachful eyes in history class, then rolled back up again after, up and up until there is more fabric—if you can call it that—bunched at the waist than there is covering our legs. Sometimes, when they unravel at the hems, we staple them back in place. The skirts mean we aren't kids anymore.

Sixth grade also means mixers with Gilman, the boys' school across the street, bigger and fancier than our school, the first country day school in the United States, all sprawling fields, serious buildings, boys with shorts the color of overripe cantaloupe, waving lacrosse sticks above their sandy blond heads like they are beckoning something from above.

"What are you wearing?" we start asking each other on Monday, in anticipation of Friday night at the Gilman gym. I can see it—boy bands piped over the loudspeaker, floors squeaking under our shoes. I'm floating up in the cyclone of my unexpected beauty, the fantasy that I will be something other than myself come Friday night.

Friday after school, we fill Steph's mom's minivan with shrieks of weekend joy, high from the possibility of our first dance with boys, sing "Mambo Number 5" along with the radio.

"Are there any cute boys?" Steph's mom cranes her neck to inquire, and we all shake our heads no. Yet against all odds, we have hope.

With the cushy end of the tube of gloss my mom bought me for my bat mitzvah, I paint my lips sticky. In the mirror, for a second, I like what I see. Steph won't let me glitter up her eyelids, but I let Amanda do my hair in an elaborate mess she calls a French twist. In the car on the way to Gilman, I untwist it in a wave of sudden insecurity.

The gym smells like cotton candy, Bonne Bell, and locker room. We drink effulgent punch and eat potato chips served in neat rows of matching plastic cups. Ms. Rosner glowers by the snack table. If she wasn't there, I would be drinking and eating as many cups of things as I could get away with, the sugar and salt a balm for my electric nerves.

Instead, we huddle on the dance floor in tight clusters. A disco ball paints us intermittently glittery. I wish I had left Amanda's twist in my hair, which now falls hot on my neck. I wish I was not me. I like my denim skirt well enough; its slit up my left thigh feels grown-up. I like the jingly bangles on my wrist.

But I hate my shirt, a tank chosen for its ability to hide the wide straps of my bra. The cool girls file in, each one in a tube top, bubble-gum pink and baby blue, no bras, no problem, matching ribbons in their ponytails. They wave their arms and their tube tops stay in place. They dance and their ponytails bounce to "I Want It That Way," ribbons rippling like flags. I readjust one set of straps to cover the other set. An hour ago, in Steph's bathroom mirror, I felt pretty, sleek. Under the disco ball, I promise myself I will never again be so stupid.

In spring of sixth grade, my class embarks on the much-anticipated immigration-themed field trip to New York City. I share headphones on the bus ride with Emily and sing along to Blink-182, letting the weight of my head fall on her fleece-clad shoulder. When we emerge from the tunnel, that arresting surge of NYC energy hits me. I drink it in, feel it in my bones. We have to sit on the bus while instructions are delivered. I'm antsy; I want out into the raucous midtown frenzy.

As field trips go, it's pretty great. We ride the ferry to Ellis Island, the wind in our hair, and wave at Miss Liberty. We visit the Tenement Museum on the Lower East Side. They let us loose in SoHo, and, for a few hours, I am the happiest eleven-year-old in the world. I make a promise to myself: I will move to New York as soon as possible. I can't think of anything better than living right here.

We plan to have lunch in Chinatown. We split up into groups and get deposited on Mott Street to choose a dining destination. I am spellbound—there are tiny turtles and chimes for sale on the sidewalk, ducks hanging morbidly by their little duck feet in the windows, bunches of greens and orb-shaped mysterious fruits, herbs that smell horrible and magical, little old men making grand plumes with stinky cigars. I can't wait for lunch.

What will we eat? Tender soup dumplings that ooze savory, salty broth? Crimson nuggets of fatty-crispy pork? Piles of pliable hand-pulled noodles studded with fiery Sichuan peppercorns?

My classmates point at the Canal Street golden arches. I assume they are joking. They are not joking.

I lay out my argument carefully: we have traveled for hours on a hot bus, only one ear of Blink-182 playing, to feast on delicacies from the one and only Chinatown, NYC. Now's our big chance to try something exotic, transformative, delicious. Big Macs and fries are perhaps a respectable lunch choice in suburban Baltimore, but here's our chance to step it up, to branch out, to have not just a meal, but an experience.

They listen politely, then line up for Mickey D's.

I cry. I try not to, but the edifice of this day is shattered. *When will I be here again?* Also, I feel lonely. *How can I be the only one to understand?* There are sixty girls in the class, but it feels as if there is no one.

Mrs. W comes to the rescue, the very nice, very quiet math teacher. She wears big glasses and long skirts. I hate math, but suddenly I adore her. She notices my distress.

"What's wrong?"

"I would really, really love to try some Chinatown Chinese food."

"So would I!"

Mrs. W whisks me away to some teeny hole-in-the-wall. It smells of salt and fat and promise; I feel my tears drying, the soft, strong hand of relief and deliciousness. We carry Styrofoam containers of steaming, juicy, crispy-skinned Peking duck piled on mounds of snow-white rice, and greens tangled with a mess of garlic and chilies back to the hard plastic McDonald's tables where we sit with my classmates and dig in. They unwrap their burgers. Everybody is happy.

Home from the field trip, my mom takes me to the mall. It's a total treat: new clothes, maybe an Orange Julius, bright and creamy and sugary enough to make the mall's fluorescent lights feel soft. Mom needs new black pants for work—her default uniform—so we head into a store for grown-ups. "This won't take too long," she promises.

I follow her, mustering my patience as she plucks a few pairs and drapes a small pile over her arm. I perch on the narrow bench in the dressing room and hold her coat in my lap while she begins to wiggle into a pair.

I watch as her smile collapses. Suddenly, the shine in her eyes goes dim.

"They don't even *almost* fit."

"What about the other pants?" I ask, hopeful.

"No way will they make it over my thighs."

"How do you know if you don't try them on?"

"I know."

We make a beeline out of the store, pantsless, defeated. This isn't the first time I've seen my mom look into the mirror with a face painted in pain.

My mom tells me about waitressing to put herself through college. About her boss who looked her up and down and declared, "You walk like an elephant. You're supposed to walk like a ballerina."

Is this why she scolds me for stepping too loudly across the moaning floorboards of our house? They are old, creaky, nearly regal. When I remember, I tiptoe. But I rarely remember, and more often the whole house brays under the weight of my ungraceful steps.

She tells me about Helen, her own mom, who died a few months before I was born. I have her Hebrew name. Helen chain-smoked and drank martinis and read libraries worth of books. She was stylish, with wrists as thin as reeds. When my mom gained weight, Helen panicked. Her criticism was razor sharp and stinging.

Mom is on a diet, off a diet. I do my homework in the back of Weight Watchers meetings, writing down the colors of the rainbow in Spanish in my workbook and half-listening to tips about tuna fish, not snacking at night.

I love when my mom goes to step class at her gym. Across the street is a bagel shop, where she leaves me with my books and my homework. I order an everything with lox and scallion cream cheese while she steps up and down and all around in her stretchy leggings and a baggy shirt. I read my book and savor the way the soft cheese smooshes between the bagel's crunchy outside. I try to make my bagel last as long as possible. When it is gone, I have lost something. I feel grown-up, hanging out alone with book and bagel. When Mom picks me up, her face is red and sweaty and her smile is huge.

"How was your bagel?"

"It was so good. I got an everything with lox! How was your workout?"

During Atkins mania, we stop eating bagels, my mom joining the collective panic that carbs are making us fat. "But bagels are my favorite," I protest. She tells me I can still eat bagels if I want, but I don't want to be fat, either. Post-Atkins, there is a new philosophy where carbs are permissible if they have a lot of fiber, so we switch to crispbreads that taste like burnt cardboard and hurt to chew. My mom serves them for breakfast with a slice of lox and a smear of cream cheese, as if they are bagels, but neither of us is fooled.

Our cabinets usually contain spices, grains, the very healthy kind of cereal that looks like pet food. Still, I open the door expectantly, hoping for a miracle snack. "Mom! We have absolutely nothing to eat."

When I visit Steph or Amanda or Jen for sleepovers, my mind explodes with the bounty of junk food: crackers, cookies, sugary cereal, chips, gummy things, chocolate goodies, rows of brightly colored packages that contain immense promise. My childhood friends' cabinets are the stuff of my wildest dreams.

Steph's kitchen is the best. It's Friday after school, and the two of us are standing in her cupboard, which is as big as my bedroom. We're still in our uniform skirts, running our fingers across the rainbow colors of the plastic packaging. We pull out bags and boxes and bring them out to the rest of the girls, who have concocted an elaborate game to read everyone's future. *Who will get married first? Who will be a celebrity in Singapore?*

But what is my future when these chips, pretzels, and candies sprawl out before me on Steph's immense dining room table? We stick our hands in for fistfuls.

"Let's bake brownies," I suggest. Steph's cupboard is stacked with mixes and potions. I have a vision: we can trick out our tray of dense brownies with extra chocolate chips and ice the whole thing with fudge sauce.

"We have to clean up or my mom will go crazy." Steph folds her arms across her unformed chest.

"Fine. Promise."

Steph gets out bowls and organizes what we need—eggs, canola oil. Amanda and Jen move from dining room to kitchen. They perch on the kitchen counter, their legs swinging. Steph supervises my measuring and mixing. I follow the directions on the box, lick the spoon. I offer the girls the last batter in the bowl, but they are indifferent, so I scrape that into my mouth, too.

The wait for the brownies to bake seems endless.

"We have to let them to cool before we frost them," Steph instructs when they're finally ready. I know she's right, but I resent her authority. I watch the chocolate chips ooze beneath the still-hot brownies.

"Well we don't have to follow the rules just because they're rules," I insist. I smear half the gummy frosting from the jar onto the brownies, which sag a little beneath the weight of my spatula. The other half of the frosting goes into my mouth. The sweetness is so sharp it burns. Sure enough, the brownies melt the icing into a puddle at the bottom of the tray. I shower sprinkles on top to try to hide the mess.

"Brownies are served!"

Amanda just looks at me quizzically. "I'll pass." I cut wedges for Steph and Jen and take a slice for myself. They're still warm and a little gluey.

After a few minutes, Steph, Jen, and Amanda lose interest in the brownies, the Cheetos and Cheez-Its and Oreos we've been nibbling. I never lose interest. I finish the last of the brownies, scraping off the icing that has hardened around the tray's edges while they move on to debating who is the most popular, or the best songs of Third Eye Blind, and weaving gigantic, serious plans for the rest of our lives: Steph is going to be a famous wedding planner and Amanda is going to be the first female NBA star and an astrophysicist on the side. I am going to write the great American novel and have my own cooking show.

My fingers grope the bottom of the bags for the last salty crumbs. When there is nothing left, I feel sadness creep into my belly. After a night of movies, whispers, gossip, and games, everyone is asleep and I am jolted awake by sugar. I lie in my sleeping bag, painting swirls on the ceiling in my mind, swoops and cityscapes and cakes tall as skyscrapers.

Spaghetti (Straps)

By the time I am in high school, I have amassed multiple years of bra shopping at the old lady lingerie store. The kind where the surly bra mistress walks in on you half-naked and proceeds without permission to rearrange your breasts in her cold and wrinkly hands. My mom has big breasts like me and is a pro in the bra shop. I am already a head taller than her. We share shoes—size ten.

But I don't want a body like my mother's. I eye my friends' lacey little bras with wonder and jealousy. Bikini tops made of mere triangles of fabric. I am so young, yet an infinite lifetime of grandma bras lies before me. They are bulky and as unsexy as girdles. I have been cast out of the light of Victoria's Secret and carefree bikinis into darkness.

My mom has a beautiful friend, brunette and thin and savvily dressed, and she shows me her post-reduction breasts in the bathroom, wiggling her sweater over her head, unhooking her bra with one hand.

"Do you want to touch them?" I don't, but I do. They are soft and slick. They sit high and proud on her chest, like two tennis balls.

That's when I know I want it. Badly.

The first doctor says, "I will see you in three years" and sends me on my way. A few steps out the door, I dissolve into sobs. Three years is eternity.

"There are so many other surgeons," my mom tells me. I cry, wetting her soft hair.

I feel enormous; a hideous monster. I dream of doing the surgery myself, taking the kitchen knife to my nipples, pulling out the insides. After, my breasts will be dainty and pert. I will be dainty and pert. I will be thin.

The second doctor is fat and white, so white he is nearly incandescent. He keeps snapping his latex gloves. There are crumbs on the edges of his big lips. He swivels around in his swivel chair until I feel dizzy. I can't remember what he says, but I remember the relief of leaving his office, my mom and I in silent agreement that we will not return.

We go with the third doctor, an ageless Asian man, impeccable in a slim, shiny suit. His office is glossy, too, all sleek furniture, tall mirrors, clean lines. We leaf through photo albums of before-and-after breasts. My mom and I pass the silicone model boobs back and forth, holding them up to my chest, trying them on for size.

"You're in good hands," he says. We let ourselves be assured by his authority. My mom signs a clipboard full of papers, and we schedule the surgery for after poetry camp. There will be a few weeks to recover before my senior year of high school starts.

The night before my surgery, I sleep over at Amanda's. I want to believe life is happening as usual. We shoot hoops at the Johns Hopkins gym, where her dad is a professor. It's summer and so the building is nearly empty, except for two security guards watching *Jerry Springer*. We join them for a few minutes on metal folding chairs, bouncing basketballs between our knees. The older security guard twirls a basketball on one finger, showing off. Amanda can make friends with anyone.

Back at her place, we make tortellini from a bag and bring our bowls back to her room. We eat early, it's still light out her window—I have to fast for twenty-four hours before the operation.

"Are you scared for tomorrow?" Amanda asks.

"I think so, but it doesn't seem real."

"I'm still jealous." Amanda is almost completely flat-chested.

"Well I'm jealous of you." It's true—I wonder what the freedom of no bra feels like, the lightness of her body.

"Maybe I can have the extra boobs that they remove, like an exchange." We laugh, but I am sad. *Are we all destined to be unhappy with our bodies?*

Amanda's still asleep when my mom picks me up from her place early in the morning. At home, I shower with special soap from the doctor that makes my skin feel itchy and raw. On the way to the hospital, my mom keeps one hand on the steering wheel and the other in mine.

The third doctor, my doctor, says he is an artist and seems to believe it. I don't have to stay in the waiting room long. He covers me in antibacterial goo, then outlines my chest in Sharpie, circling the nipples, a painter lovingly prepping his canvas.

That is the first time I comprehend the physicality of what lies ahead. The surgery had seemed an idea, a concept. Sweet transformation. Now it is here, in Sharpie, on my skin, which feels scalding.

There will be knives and scalpels. I will be slit and emptied. The room fades to little dots. It spins in imperfect, bumpy circles. I feel wet and cold and excruciatingly hot. I need to sit down.

After the surgery, there is less pain than an enormous feeling of pressure, as if a truck has rolled atop my chest and stayed there. With every breath, it reasserts its presence.

Days pass, and the pressure recedes into a dull throb. At night, I try to sleep on my back. When I roll over, the pain startles me. The incisions itch wildly. There are blood-filled drains to be emptied, bandages to be changed. I avert my eyes resolutely when my mom plays nurse in our bathroom. I study the clean tiled walls.

"Don't you want to see?" she asks. I do not. The mirror is enemy number one.

When I look, on day number three or four, pulling up my shirt to face down the mirror, my tummy reacts first. It feels punched, hard and quick. The devastation is sour in my mouth. The skin is bruised and swollen, a patchwork of blood and brown and ravage. Everything is wrong.

Post recovery, spaghetti straps are the first order of business. They were the telos for the surgery, the emblem of everything I wanted to be and was not: thin, beautiful. With F cups and bra straps as wide as seat belts, spaghetti straps were not an option. I saw them in my future, shiny and bright—deliverance. Scars and anesthesia and many thousands of my parents' dollars were nothing. I would have sold my soul for spaghetti straps. I don't even dare hope for a tube top. Such towering aspirations seem greedy.

We decided—my surgeon, my mom, and I—that at five foot nine and a bit, with plenty of curve in my hips and broad shoulders, I shouldn't go too tiny. My right boob was a little bigger, but no longer. My artist surgeon worked his magic in such a way that my breasts became perkier. Sixteen-year-old boobs should be fabulously sprightly but mine had been pendulous and funkily shaped. After surgery, they are round as the earth, rimmed in pink, puckered scars, perfectly symmetrical.

Still, the "after" picture is all wrong. I don't become skinny and tiny. The spaghetti straps are a pipe dream. When I go back to school for senior year, nobody notices. If they do, they are silent. I feel the devastation in my chest, my bones, their marrow. I am still me.

"You look the same, pretty much," Amanda tells me. "But that's not a bad thing. I still want your boobs."

I leave calculus class and cry in a bathroom stall.

When I go to wash my hands and my face, Astor is painting her lips glossy. The fluorescent lights have turned my tears a garish yellow. I try to wipe away the evidence with a scratchy paper towel. "Whatever it is, it'll get better," Astor says to my reflection. I can't tell if she's being dismissive or sweet. But it will get better, I know it. I will escape from this place to college in New York. It has been my plan since forever, but the end of high school is so close I can almost touch it. In my dazzling future, I will never see Astor again, her posse, the inside of a dance studio.

Senior year is lonely. Amanda spends more time with her older boyfriend, and Steph has new friends from the lacrosse team. I want a boyfriend more than anything.

I write poetry on the benches outside our lockers, filling absurd numbers of notebooks with long, loopy lines.

> *Our words refused sleep and other tidal waves*
> *itched our footsoles, mocked our promises, trashed*
>   *our souvenirs*
> *shined our hair glorious, swam on their bellies in the*
>   *puddles of our tears.*

I read. No matter how lonely I feel, how much an outsider, how fat, I am welcome in the world of words, stories, poems. They hold my hand. They show me that there are more ways to think and feel than I may fathom. The world takes on new contours; colors become more vivid.

I study, making myself so anxious about the test on the Crimean War that I sleep with my textbooks, waking up to look up the Siege of Sevastopol, the Ottomans twirling their long guns around in my brain, bruising my skull with their barrels.

The test is so important because college is so important. College means everything. If my body is one measure of my self-worth, college is the other. All of my life's work, my blood, sweat, tears, my head, my heart will be validated by an acceptance letter. Or vice versa.

I set my sights on Columbia. It's an easy decision, really. The Ivy League means the world will nod in assent. In my mind, I am already debating elbow-patched professors in Literature Humanities about the *Inferno*'s third circle of hell, where gluttons are forced to linger in a slush of ceaseless, foul sleet. Everyone is smart at Columbia and nobody ties pastel ribbons in their hair. In my fantasy, something remarkable happens at college. I am not an outsider. I belong.

New York makes me swoon, too, wide-eyed. In New York, not everyone looks the same, has the same dreams, plays lacrosse in salmon-colored shorts and polos. Huge things are possible. I visit the Columbia campus, sit outside of Lerner Hall and watch the parade of people carrying piles of books, weird hair colors and the whir of traffic on Broadway. I choke on disappointment when it's time to go home.

I do everything I think might help me get in. I fence, even though I am afraid of the *thwop* of the sabre across my chest through the hard plastic bras we wear, like helmets for our breasts. I love cooking and start the Culinary Society. I think creating a club will demonstrate my ambition, leadership skills.

The club meets in my parents' kitchen, braising garlicky greens, blasting music, baking cupcakes. I love filling the kitchen with smells, sounds of chopping and sizzling, bowls of pasta, legs swinging off the countertop.

My crush Benji shows up with his pasta maker under his arm. We crack eggs into a pile of flour on the counter. Benji fishes out a piece of yolk with his pinkie finger. He feeds our dough through the mouth of the pasta machine, cranking its handle. I try to talk to him about school but he ignores me; he's laser focused on the pasta.

"It's too thick," he says of the patchy noodles that come out.

"Let me try." Nothing seems better, at this moment, than making pasta with Benji. I think this may be my chance to win him over. Steph has lost interest and is reading a magazine. Annie is frosting a cupcake pink. There are girls here from the sophomore class who I don't know too well, passing around a single bowl and a whisk.

"That's okay, I got it," Benji says, turning his back toward me. Benji smells of onions and sweat. It's like we're on a sports team and he is guarding me from his pasta maker. I realize he doesn't want me to touch his appliance. It's coated in eggy flour. The music has stopped playing.

I get a pot down from above the sink and he cooks the noodles until they're mush. The pasta sucks, but it's me who feels like a failure.

"It's not bad," I lie to Benji.

After the club goes home, I fight with my mom about the mess. We have promised to clean but have done only the most slipshod of jobs.

"I'll do it in the morning," I say. I'm used to waking up at crazy hours to study.

"But I am cooking dinner tonight, and I need to use the kitchen."

"Fine." I wipe the grimy counters and throw away our concoctions. I think, *This time next year I will be gone. Everything will be different.*

All of high school is one big hustle. I edit the literary magazine. We meet in the English classroom after school and spread our poems across the floor. Some are terrible and some are passable, but I love reading them all, the words sparkly as jewelry. The words can say more than I can. I know they will be my salvation.

I intern for my congressman in his district office in a low-slung building off the highway for so long that he thinks I am an employee. I sort through his mail until the anthrax scare forces the operation off-premises. I print out letters of congratulations for Boy Scouts, stamp them with the congressional seal, twirl around in my twirly office chair, kick off my new pumps that I picked out to make me look professionally sleek. The realization that I am still me, just with smooshed toes, teetering when I walk back and forth to the fax machine, is another cruelty.

All the activities. All the studying. I am proving something to myself. I am trying so very hard to prove it.

It's the first savage cold day of senior year, after school. I'm on my way to fencing practice when I pass the school guidance counselor in the hallway.

"Hannah, check your email."

"I'm on my way to fencing practice. I will right after."

"If I were you, I would do it now."

I slide into the computer lab, wiggle in my plastic gear. There is an email from Columbia.

> *Congratulations! It is our pleasure to inform you that you have been accepted to the Columbia College of the Columbia University of the City of New York class of 2009 . . .*

I jump up and down and up and down—my dream school, my dream. I try to play it cool in fencing practice but I can't stop smiling. I will recreate myself, embark on my new, shiny, fabulous NYC life. I will be reborn. And so: a diet.

Gelato

I diet with zeal, and for the first time, my efforts work. I rechannel the single-minded effort I had spent doing-everything-right-so-as-to-get-into-college into planning all my meals, skating along the elliptical machine, counting points, feeling hungry, calculating and recalculating when and where I may achieve skinnydom. I eat a lot of apples. I weigh myself on Thursday mornings, first thing, before I have eaten anything. I think breakfast may nudge the scale in the wrong direction. Wednesday nights, I can't sleep, my mouth sour with worry about what the scale will tell me. Thursday morning, I eat. If I'm thinner, I feel I have earned it. If not, the food tastes soggy with defeat.

At college in New York, life is going to start, and it is going to be grand. I am going to be a whole new Hannah. Like myself, but immensely better.

Skinnier, of course. Skinnier is everything. Skinniness is next to godliness.

My parents and I move from our house to an apartment in Hoboken the day after my high school graduation. I don't know a soul. The first night, we order whole wheat pasta from an Italian place, garlic bread, broccoli rabe, but I'm still hungry. After my mom and dad close the door to their bedroom at night, I eat a whole box of granola bars in my old bed, within this new apartment. I can't stop myself. I make a mess of granola crumbs and hot tears on the pillow. My new life is full of possibility but I am stuck inside myself. My stomach feels round and big as the moon.

I have big plans for my summer. I want to do unambitious things like make eight bucks an hour scooping ice cream, read a lot of trashy mags, and sleep. It sounds wild, an adventure. Also, I will diet. When I start my new life at Columbia in the fall, I plan to have a stomach flat as the sidewalk, thighs that don't rub together, leaving the skin between them raw and itchy.

I sign up for a commercial diet program and count my food. It doesn't feel like enough, not even close, but hunger seems a small price to pay for liking myself, for not dreaming of carving away the flesh below my belly button, the sides of my butt.

The morning after my granola bar binge, I set out to diet harder. Also, I need a summer job.

I meet Corey in the first five minutes of my job search. There is a shiny new restaurant with an orange awning right outside the PATH station, mere blocks from my parents' new Hoboken apartment. First, I see his hostess staring somewhere way past me, unfathomably bored. I have a résumé and a blazer, which feels tight around my shoulders.

"May I speak to a manager? I came to see about job opportunities."

The hostess rolls her eyes and disappears. Then there is Corey in his chef whites, a smile that contains its own conversation. He saunters over. His skin is tanned and his eyes are sunny, like he has just returned from surfing. He shakes my hand and offers me a fountain soda.

We sit at the glossy table, sipping from straws. It doesn't feel like an interview. I learn that we are both poets: I have won some national high school poetry contest, he has half of a master's degree, a little less.

Corey quotes Bukowski, "Some people never go crazy. What truly horrible lives they must lead." Neither of us lives horrible lives, I think.

When he smiles at me, I feel like the cool girls must feel. His light shines on me and I am warm in its glow.

I learn Corey runs this business for his dad. Even so, they are having a fight and not speaking.

"He's an asshole, but he's my dad. You know how it is." I nod like I know.

It is Corey's thirty-eighth birthday. My eighteenth birthday is in September. I think, *Nearly twenty years*. Twenty years is boundless.

"I was just thinking of opening a little gelato bar outside for the summer. And now you're here on my birthday. It's a sign."

"I could scoop gelato. I really like gelato."

Corey's smile takes up all his face, his body. I feel it; the adventure is starting.

And thus concludes my job search. I return the next day, roll out Corey's new ice cream cart to the patio, wipe it with a bleach-soaked rag until it shines. We debate: mint chocolate chip or chocolate chip cookie dough. He buys me a racehorse of a scooper: "Look at that baby." I run it through our first container of vanilla bean, scoop up a perfect sphere.

I find a rhythm. Roll out cart, wipe cart obsessively, count my cash, wait, wait, read, wait. Sell a scoop.

I like the hazelnut the best; it tastes like secrecy, like the promise that more will be revealed. "The gelato is not for the staff," Corey tells me, but he fills up quart containers with strawberry and vanilla when the line is slow, the pink melting down the sides, hands out cups to the menacing meat cook and the rest of his crew.

"Hi, gelato girl," they tell me, but Corey looks at them hard and they stop.

When the place is slow, which is often, too often, Corey comes outside to chat. My job is lonely—the gelato biz isn't going so well—and I like his stories. They are good distractions, and Corey tells them with his whole body, as if nothing could be more important. He tells me about cooking lobster for his girlfriend in a giant pot. It was the best lobster money could buy, purchased on the down-low from a seafood dealer, boiled alive in said pot and served with a bowlful of drawn butter and candlelight. "That bitch stole my pot," he tells me.

There are stories about whether or not to keep the girlfriend, whom I imagine is blonde and wears pastel polo shirts and smiles rarely. She hates Corey's windy stories. I never meet her or even see her in a photo, but she is as clear to me as a close friend. Story still unfinished, he resumes laughing with one of our regulars or barking at his dad on the phone in his swivelly office chair, feet up, door closed.

I make up the end to the stories myself. I wonder what Corey writes about, if his poems have neat, terse lines or swoop across the page.

I try not to let him see me read, which I do all day. I read *Kitchen Confidential*, and it blows my mind. I long for the kitchen adventure. I want to cook on a line, adrenaline hot in my veins. But it's okay, at least for today, with my book and my gelato cart.

It is really, really slow in the sticky New Jersey summer. Gelato customers are scarce. I am not used to being bored, not good at it. I crack my fingers. The heat churns my stomach. I spin elaborate details of the lives of the moms who pass by with strollers, teenagers in short, short shorts. I write lines of poems on napkins. The ones I like get scrunched into my uniform pockets, the rest go in the trash can with gelato tasting cups and plastic spoons.

Corey is squinty eyed, olive skinned, gorgeous. Unbearably cool in a way I know I will never be. He walks in long strides. Seeing him makes me feel like I know some wildly good news.

"Punch out," Corey says, a week into my new job. It's only early afternoon and I feel like I've been standing watch at the gelato cart for days. The restaurant is slow and I have only sold one cup of strawberry. I am too spaced out to write my napkin poetry. We walk together to the park across the street, the Manhattan skyline, drunk on its own beauty, the outrageous summer sunshine, gaudy.

"Do you smoke?" He passes me a joint, his face near my face, holds up a light. The heat is immense, as if his skin is all lit up. His cheek rests against my cheek for a moment, soft, and I stop breathing for a few beats. He takes the joint, inhales as if he were about to disappear under water, then holds it up for me, his fingers dry against my lips. When I get back to work I am no longer bored. The sky is translucent like ice.

I spend the rest of the summer traveling between the gelato stand and Corey's apartment.

Come over, he texts at all hours of the night. *Just wanna cuddle.* I don't mind the lie.

I stop writing poems. I lie to my parents about where I'm going, only half-wondering if they believe me.

I read Corey's books: Henry Miller, Frank O'Hara. *I am the least difficult of men. All I want is boundless love.*

We watch movies, get high and giggly or high and sad. By July, the girlfriend returns his big pot, leaves it outside his apartment door, and is not mentioned again.

"At least you're eighteen," Corey tells me one day at work. I am helping him in the kitchen, wrapping chocolate chip cookies in little bags. We're alone, his baseball hat backward, brown hair peeking out around his ears. He looks younger than thirty-eight, I think, despite the deep creases around his vast eyes. The cookies are still warm, chips melty, taunting me. I feel the flesh of my stomach against the waistband of my scratchy black uniform pants, vow the cookies will never touch my lips, want them, want Corey, want so much my muscles ache.

I tell him the truth.

"You're fucking with me."

"Why would I do that? You saw my driver's license when you hired me."

"Why would I pay attention?"

"Why would you assume I'm eighteen?"

"Think about it." I'm already thinking; my thoughts make me seasick.

This is the first time I feel Corey's acid anger directed toward me. His eyes turn shrively, like old raisins, and he averts them when I pass by at work that afternoon. I keep looking at my phone. Usually he texts all day, every day. It's been three straight days of silence, now four, and each yawns and stretches, absurdly long. Still, I keep looking at my phone's blank screen, waiting for him to change his mind. At work, he's holed up in his office or nowhere to be found.

In my parents' Hoboken apartment, my childhood mattress feels too soft, like I'm going to sink into the ether. I have notebooks full of what I'm eating and not eating. Without Corey, the pages taunt me. Maybe he's angry because I'm too fat. I hate the way my thighs brush together under my summer skirts. I hate my reflection on the slick glass of my gelato cart.

"I have to talk to you." I touch his arm. We're at work and he looks far away. His arms are muscly, strong, and they make my heart hurt. It has been five days, but feels like five months. "In your office. Please." It scares me, how much I miss him. My stomach feels itchy, empty.

He shuts the door behind him, exhales. His hands look smaller, there is a swath of purple under his eyes.

I make my case. "What's the big deal? There's nothing illegal about it. I looked it up. The age of legal consent in New Jersey is sixteen, fifteen in New York. It's cool. I'm cool. I've always, always been precocious. Everyone thinks I'm older, and in a way I am. I feel old. Ancient. And I'll be eighteen in a month. I don't understand why this is so important. It's not my fault, my age."

"You don't get it," he says.

"Maybe I don't. I want to."

"You don't."

I think about how little I know this man, all big ideas and roller-coaster moods. How little he knows me.

"Come home with me today," he finally says.

And I do.

Once, before we slept together, Corey asked me if I was a virgin. We were sitting on his windowsill, where we always sat to smoke joints and breathe the still air on 77th Street. The question offended me. Corey was full of secrets and I wanted to be like that: impenetrable. I told him no.

A few months before, the end of high school approaching, I had sex with a friend who played the sax. He was not sexy, not to me, but I wanted to have sex, and he proposed it, a transaction. It seemed like another thing to get out of the way, check off my list. I didn't want to go to college a virgin, or to imbue sex with the excessive weight of meaning. And I wanted to see what all the fuss was about.

Waiting for him, I ran the razor across my legs so hard they turned red. I conference-called Steph and Amanda on the phone, which was shaky in my hand.

Amanda was dating a short Italian with a juicy accent and chest hair that sprang forth from the gaps between his shirt buttons. Steph's boyfriend had graduated from Gilman, and she drove to his UVA dorm to see him, where they had lots of sex in the library stacks and serious conversations in the rain. I felt late to the game.

"The first time was the worst." Amanda loves some good drama. Her voice was faraway on speaker phone. "I thought he was going to break me. I almost punched him in the face. But it gets better. I'm fine now. Tell him to go slow."

"Get a towel," Steph said. "Put it under the sheets. It'll hurt, but he'll think you're screaming in pleasure. Good luck, girl."

It wasn't much better than that.

The next day, the sax player asked for a blow job in his new beige car, on some curvy road we were driving down, just because. I said *okay, why not*, if I was going to have sex for the first time, I may as well do this for the first time, too. But it was not a whole minute with his long, skinny dick in my mouth before I puked. I managed to open the door, so only a trickle sullied his new car upholstery, beige on beige.

"Jesus," he said, not kindly. "Let me drive you home."

Corey is my first lover. Everything is different. We write each other pieces of poems, I save the stanzas on crumpled napkins. He leaves me lines on scraps of paper in little piles under my ice cream scooper. We dance with our hipbones touching or almost touching. His hands on my neck, my hair, my back: it seems the most magnificent thing.

With Corey, the sex is intense, thrilling. I lose myself in it. I get the fuss. I feel transformed, giddy. Time folds in on itself. He puts his hand up my skirt in his office, bends me over, his palm over my mouth. It is the best drug—wanting him, him wanting me. The room spins.

I am scared to show him the scars that pucker around my boobs— they are pinkish and angry. But he says "I think they're sexy" and kisses the bull's-eye they make around each nipple. I am confounded. Perhaps nothing is as it seems.

So much better than being cool, I feel powerful. My skin and bones are different, electric. When he touches my leg, my leg feels tingly, feels not like my leg at all. He is the puppeteer making me move, and croon, and shimmy, the strings dancing in his big hands.

I still hate the roundness of my belly, pull on the flesh around my hips and fantasize about its evisceration. But I have felt immense pleasure and given the same. The power of that straightens my spine.

One day I come to work in a fire engine–red skirt, my scratchy black uniform scrunched into my purse.

"Don't change," Corey says. "You look amazing. I want to look at you in that skirt."

"What about my uniform?"

"I'm your boss. Screw the uniform."

This sounds horrifying, being crimson in a sea of black, and I head to the bathroom and zip up my issued polyester pants, pull the sleeves up on my cotton uniform shirt. The way men look at me sometimes, now, the way Corey looks at me, makes my stomach seize. *Is this what I've wanted?* I can't decide. There is a flattering element, but it swims around with blinding, ragged fear. I am Corey the lion's prey. I want to bolt. And I want his fangs around my smooth-skinned neck, my blood on his chin.

"Always wear that red skirt," he tells me later, stepping out for a cigarette. The sun casts its summer rage on my black-clad skin. I feel sticky, trapped. I never pull the skirt over my hips again, although it hangs in my closet. Sometimes I finger its silky sheen, considering.

One day, after work at the gelato shop, I ride the PATH to the West Village for no reason, to walk among the twisty blocks and peer in fancy restaurants and dark pubs. One of those ubiquitous New York summer street fairs snakes through the streets, stalls of cheap earrings and sunglasses, kebabs and corn licked by flames, big baskets and rolled-up rugs. I stop to look at a vendor selling racks of flowy skirts, one has a diagram—a gazillion ways to tie it into a dress, a sarong, one shoulder, no shoulders, like magic.

There is a guy, nerdy looking, sad, on the other side of the rack. He peers over, and we make eye contact.

"Hi," he says.

"Hi."

"You're very beautiful, like a model."

"Thanks." His eyes are wider than they should be, all pupils, like he's taken an opiate. His gaze feels like a scratch on my skin, unbearable. I leave the flowy skirt stand, make a beeline past the MozzArepas and the pickle guys. There he is, still.

"Can we talk?"

"No, I have to go."

I duck into a bodega, wanting him badly to go away already, feeling like I may liquefy into the summer heat. I feel my heart thrum in my chest, quick and jagged. There he is by the fridge of beer, the rolls of Pringles. He doesn't say anything this time, his eyes are hard on me.

I leave fast. My flip-flops flop onto Christopher Street and down into the whoosh of the PATH station. I look 360 degrees around. I see a group of teenagers, an old couple, holding hands in the refrigerator-cold train car. He is gone, my breath heavy in my chest.

I think, *This is because of my diet.* Fifteen pounds ago, this would never have happened. *Is this what people want? Why?*

Back in Hoboken, I head up the stairs, the summer air fat with heat, and see the orange awning above my empty gelato stand, a cook smoking outside, arms and legs crossed, the smoke wafting into the sun.

Corey's hunger is its own animal. It comes and goes. He wants me, and then he wants nothing to do with me. It is volatile like my own. And it is totally different. It scares me, and fascinates me, and intoxicates me.

I don't throw up sucking his dick. He spends a lot of time telling me what to do, as if he's giving directions to an obscure location.

"Act like you don't know what you are doing, or guys will think you're a slut." I wonder if this is what he thinks of me. What he thinks of me seems both urgent and beside the point.

Corey tells me to lose weight. We are smoking in his windowsill, and I am high in that way that everything feels poignant—the church on West End across the street with its spire rising up so hopefully, the way Corey's muscly chest rises and falls when he breathes.

"Your face is a ten, but your body is a six," he says, unprompted. "I'm only grading you harshly because you have such potential. You could be a ten, even, if you lost some weight, got in great shape."

I feel as if my skin has been peeled from me. And yet, I agree. I have always been trying to shrink myself, fix myself, a project not so much of self-improvement but obliteration. Corey's words sound like the truth.

"I wish I didn't love food so much," I tell him. I can think of nothing more satisfying than turning overripe bananas into soft banana bread, folding in chocolate chips, licking my fingers, watching the alchemy of its rising. Scrambling eggs, roasting chicken studded with an obscene amount of garlic. Even now, in this awful moment.

Food, my great love, my great tormenter.

"Just lose some weight, then you can go back to loving food."

The next morning, Corey makes us sandwiches on flaky croissants: egg and fatty pancetta, a grind of pepper. We eat them rapturously.

That's it, I think after, *until I lose the weight*. My last meal.

I buy new clothes. People say "you look great" with a lot of feeling. When my parents drive me to my cinder-block dorm room in Morningside Heights, I have lost twenty pounds, maybe twenty-five, and have another thirty to go, or rather, an immense and eternal amount. I feel light, a new gap between my thighs, my bras are baggy around my boobs. And I feel heavy, too: monstrous, not worthy of my new and shiny life. Trapped, still, in myself.

And yet. Everything is blindingly bright with possibility. My mom and dad cry, and so do I.

Gorp

Before college starts, I have orientation. And before orientation, I have a backpacking trip.

It's called COHOP, Columbia Outdoor Hiking Orientation Program. We all gather on the campus great lawn to prepare for the trip, and the first thing I do is meet Ursula. She's as tall as I am—I always notice women as tall as I am—and skinnier, all silky jet-black hair, muscly calves, and a smart kind of piercing beauty.

The plan is to set up our sleeping bags on the bright grass in front of Butler Library, spend the first night there, then depart at the crack of dawn. I feel the hot creep of anxiety. It's not that I miss Corey, but his absence feels like the sun burning my already-burnt skin, unbearable.

The organizers hand out army-green packs and split us into hiking foursomes: I am to brave the wilderness with Ryan, a surly engineer with white-blond hair; Rico, a statistics genius from Spanish Harlem, who will get recruited for the Mets way before graduation; and, thankfully, Ursula.

"Oh my god, I'm so glad you're in my group," she says.

"I was thinking the same thing." We break into nervous smiles. She has a twinkle in her eye.

"I backpacked alone through Ecuador last summer." I am immediately jealous. "It was nothing like this."

Urs and I fall in friend-love at first sight. We don't stop talking. We have both chosen Columbia because we want to live in Manhattan, and here we are, about to head out into the middle of nowhere. Like college freshmen everywhere: defensive, bewildered, thrilled.

The COHOP people round us up on the great lawn—an expanse of green covered in a battalion of eighteen-year-olds, the statue *Alma Mater*'s arms open and glistening in the end-of-summer sun. Someone teaches us the school song, which we all promptly forget and never utter again, and then we pack for our weeklong backpacking expedition into the deep, dark Catskills.

We need to pack sleeping bags and tents and tarps, but my team is most concerned with the food. This is a relief; I feel less alone. On the lawn sit humungous piles of apples, jars of peanut butter, hot dogs, bags of beans, and vast seas of hummus.

Menu planning is supposed to be a team-building experience—figure out what you need for the week, be strategic—and we are failing.

"We're bringing the apples," Urs decides.

"We don't need all those apples," Ryan argues.

"Personally, I eat a lot of apples." I am suddenly afraid we will starve in the mountains. We can't bear to part with our giant stick of pepperoni or our boxes of rice, and so we take more than the recommended load, stuffing our smelly packs 'til the seams groan.

"We have rice. We have beans. But we have no plantains," Rico says. "We absolutely need plantains. I have the best recipe."

Our foursome agrees. When we start laughing—Rico, Urs and I, Ryan even joins in, for a moment—it's the salve of cool breeze. We decide we cannot begin our trek without plantains.

The COHOP rules are clear—we are not to leave campus. Under the cover of Morningside Heights night, the four of us sneak out. We giggle up Amsterdam Avenue, proud of our rebellion. Rico knows where to go. At the bodega, we don't stop at plantains. Avocados! Limes! Jalapeños! We have culinary aspirations; we are becoming a team.

The next day, my group stands out. We start up the trail with bushels of plantains tied to our backs. We are going to hike, and then we are going to feast.

In our culinary ambition, we have failed to realize the mountainness of the Catskills. During the drive from New York City, they look like the kindest, gentle, rolling hills, dense with tree smell and studded with wide, clear lakes. Now, with forty pounds on our backs not including plantains, the slopes feel punishingly immense. We huff and puff and try to conceal just how out of breath we are.

Urs and I eat GORP (possibly an acronym for "good ol' raisins and peanuts" and definitely a word we say as much as possible). Green trees shoot up into the baby-blue sky. Fistfuls of chocolate chips and salted peanuts go down easy in the tonic of mountain air.

My body is constantly hungry, aching with it. I've decided to take a break from my diet during this trip, and everything I eat tastes bright and auspicious. Apples. Energy bars. GORP.

"Be careful with that GORP," Ryan interrupts his silence to tell us.

"Don't worry," Urs says. "We'll save plenty for you."

"That's not what I mean. Keep going at it like that and you're going to get fat."

"Fuck you," she says, and we laugh, but my feet feel heavy in my boots as they take me up and up and up the earth.

At the top of the day's peak, we unhook our packs, liberate ourselves, spreading our bodies over the big, round bellies of boulders. Urs and I can't stop talking about who we are and who we want to be, New York City and the choking fear of ambition, falling for the wrong people, starting over. Urs is a music composer and also a scientist. She plays the piano, harp, and viola. Other instruments, too, but she's just messing around with those. She's brilliant, but it's her laugh that makes me love her. She gets it. She has an ex-girlfriend that she still dreams about, a violin player with hands calloused from practice. The boys roll their eyes at us and go off to pitch our tents. When they disappear into the brush, I tell Urs about Corey. She has her own Corey, a music teacher who has a daughter our age.

"He still sends me letters every month, without fail, declaring his undying love," she says. "And gifts on Christmas and my birthday: chocolates, stuffed animals, cheesy things."

"That's sweet. Or is it creepy?"

"A little bit of both, with an emphasis on the creepy."

"How long were you together?"

"We weren't *together*. But we hooked up. And I was a little bit obsessed with him, maybe for a year. And then I met his daughter and she kind of reminded me of myself and the whole thing freaked me out."

"I'm sorry. That sounds so hard." Of course I relate.

"Now he disgusts me."

"I think I'm in love with Corey."

"I wonder if that's the pattern. First love. Then disgust."

We stretch our arms out wide over the boulders, the world far away, below us, inconsequential.

Ryan lights the camp stove. I get the rice and beans started, cut the starchy plantains into rough slabs with my not-so-sharp Swiss army knife. The stove proves uncooperative. Everyone is hunched over its unmighty flame. We prod it and blow gently and change the canister and change it back. Barely, pathetically, the beans bubble. Even with the GORP and energy bars and apples, our bellies rumble. My legs feel gelatinous from countless miles under the weight of my pack.

We mash up our avocados and jalapeños, squeeze our lime. The guacamole is a revelation—smooth and rich as butter. We scoop up the mess with already-stale tortillas, and in just a moment, it is gone.

Our main course is gloopy, still raw. The sun sets lazily behind a mountain, our feet achy. The pine breeze feels so generous, so good in my lungs.

We have two senior "guides," a hipster art student and a rugby player.

"You guys." They remind us of our one-hour camping training. "Leave no trace. We can't leave our dinner here. And bears."

But we can't stomach the mash that was our dinner.

So we play all kinds of games on our mountain—eating games, where the losers have to shovel in bites of nearly-raw beans and al dente rice and still-hard plantains. It is dark and the sky is spattered with starlight and still, there is a heaping bowl of our food-failure left.

"Can we bury it?"

"No. Bears!"

The moon shines, and fireflies fire, and we build a small fire, carefully, which becomes a slightly larger fire, into which we throw the congealing remains.

Everyone curls into their plastic tents, but Urs and I can't stop talking. We lie on our backs, the earth solid beneath us. We talk about what we will eat when we return to civilization: waffles, whipped cream, watermelon, and the soft-sticky-sweet plantains from La Caridad. ("You haven't had them?" Ursula blurts. "Oh my god, I'm taking you as soon as we get back.") The stars, they croon us love songs.

In the morning, there are charred pieces of beans that we scatter into the woods. Then, we pack up and head up the next mountaintop, munching on thick, salty slices of pepperoni and more GORP, which we finish without sharing . . . everything ahead of us.

Urs and I go to the diner for milkshakes and those waffles when we get home.

I text Corey that I'm back.

"You know you don't have to see him anymore, right?" Urs tells me. She is the voice of reason. But oh, I do.

Corey continues to wear cargo shorts when the leaves begin to fall from the trees. Now that I'm in college and no longer live in my parents' place, I can spend the night with him without anyone worrying about me. I have a single dorm room near Urs's, with a furry blanket on my twin bed and a collage of poster freebies from Chelsea art galleries. I love it. It is all mine.

But most nights, I'm with Corey. Weeks pass inside the unadorned white walls of his Upper West Side apartment. Sometimes I walk all the way from 77th Street to campus for class. I take my midterms. We buy apples and forget about them, their skins turning loose and brown.

We have sex for days in a row, and then he doesn't touch me, sits on the faraway edge of his low sofa.

"Are you ever going to meet Ursula?" I ask Corey. He's promised to take us out.

"Is she hot?" he asks, and suddenly I know what Ursula meant when she talked about disgust.

"Do you see the way men look at you?" Corey asks. "Like they're hungry?"

He has just picked me up from campus in some shiny car that isn't his. He is borrowing it, he says. He kisses me fast, palms my kneecap. The night is October cool, beckoning. I haven't eaten anything today, and the sun has gone down in a cloudless sky. My stomach gurgles, struggling against its own emptiness, and I am proud.

I have been waiting for him on Amsterdam, outside the dark of my cinder-block dorm room, when he pulls up. He is driving too fast. His eyes shine like a broken moon. We drive across Central Park, windows down, to the sound of the traffic.

"Where do you want to go?" he asks, but we end up at Westside Market to get treats that he'll eat back on his couch, like always. I'll have a bite and immediately regret it. I don't want what he suggests—slices of cheesecake and red velvet with gleaming frosting.

"You can cheat sometimes," he says, talking about the food, but I know it is not so simple.

We head to get diet soda and there behind the stacks of seltzer bottles is a boy from my Literature Humanities class, blond, glasses, hipster tight pants. I want to duck into the freezer aisle but it's too late, he's seen me.

"Hannah!" His basket is full of grapes and ice cream. "What are you up to down here?"

"Just gorging on junk food." Corey is behind me, holding our basket, which he's filled with the cakes I don't want. He looks like he's seen an alien. "This is Corey."

"Hi Corey, I'm Jack."

In the grim light of the grocery store, Corey looks like an old man. I notice the creases in his forehead, the way his hairline is receding. I am embarrassed for all of us. For a beat, we all stand in silence.

"Well, see you in class," Jack says and makes a beeline for the register. I wonder what it would be like to date Jack, his round face. He's my age but next to Corey, he looks like a baby. Dating an old(er) man is thrilling, wonderful, and weird. Something feels safe about it. Corey's judgment matters yet doesn't matter; he is not my peer, he comes from a different time, a different world.

Back at his place, Corey falls asleep on the couch as he does most nights, usually his arm slung around me, or sometimes not. He wakes me, 2 AM or 4 AM or 6 AM. "I need to go for a walk. I need you to come with me." He ties his scarf around my neck, and we walk and walk down Riverside Drive, the wind whistling. He tells stories with punch lines missing. Mostly I listen. He has no patience for my stories. The trees light up in their autumnal majesty, then the leaves start to fall, crunch beneath our feet.

"You look really skinny," he says. I have lost a pound a week, sometimes two or three, since the summer. I go long stretches of days with only Pink Lady apples, coffees with skim milk and Splenda, liters of diet soda and seltzer water. A frozen yogurt, sometimes. With sprinkles if I'm feeling extravagant. I notice my bones: collarbones, cheekbones. They are rising, it seems, up and up. My butt hurts when I sit, and sometimes my knees buckle under the weight of my body, like it's heavier in its thinness.

My new body does not feel like my own. I touch my elbows, pointy as screwdrivers. I avoid my eyes in the mirror in Corey's bathroom.

"Are you not eating carbs or just not eating?"

"The latter." I don't see any purpose in lying. I wonder if he thinks I'm doing it for him. I think about the pancetta sandwich he cooked me, the cruel extravagance of the buttery croissant.

"Be careful," he warns. "I cannot help you with this."

I get it, then, that he will never see me. I can mold myself like wet clay, hours on the elliptical. Still, we are immensely far away. My chest hurts with each inhale, the empty ache of not-enoughness.

"Are you ready for winter in New York?" he asks. I buy a parka with a fake fur collar. I study for my first semester final exams on his couch, the first finals of college, TV drone bouncing off the walls, Plato's *Symposium* all dog-eared in my lap. Corey is a secret from everyone but Urs.

Only Urs knows about Corey, and they never meet each other. He is my tricky secret.

Corey grows stubble, kisses me like he is somewhere else.

My legs are skinnier than ever and always cold. My thighs don't touch. It seems a weird battle to have won. I am supposed to be happy now, sparkly, float through the streets of New York like laughter. But deep inside my internal organs, there are millions of pounds of longing. This is not the way I thought skinniness would feel.

Corey holds my face in his hands less. The puppeteer has grown restless, changed careers. I stretch on his carpet, downward dog. My new body fascinates me. He is asleep on the couch.

On Corey's bed, the mattress sags. I awake to panic. There are no more half-poems. My loneliness nearly chokes me.

Corey quits his job, calls his father an asshole, is going to open a club in the East Village, and then is no longer going to open a club. He teaches housewives to scuba dive. He does push-ups in front of the TV. He goes out for a night, sometimes two. He talks about moving to Miami or Berlin.

"New York gets so cold in winter," he says, like he is already far away.

Ursula and I are on Riverside Drive on our way for frozen yogurt when a black-coated man pushes a gun into my side. It's dusk and he's come from nowhere. "Give me your money," he says, all breathy, and I'm so shocked I push my purse at him. He can have whatever he wants. Ursula runs. She calls 911 from the next corner.

"Not your purse," he barks. "I said your money, your money."

My hands are so quaky it's hard to get my wallet from my bag, but I do. I offer it up to him.

"Money! Not your wallet, you idiot. Your money." His voice is urgent and angry. I realize I only have a single twenty. I don't want to die.

"I'm sorry." I am crying now. I manage to pull the bill from the fold. It's slightly crumpled. The man takes it and disappears into Riverside Park.

Ursula is back, suddenly. She hugs me. It's getting dark. We are dizzy with relief.

"Were you trying to buy drugs?" the police officer asks me at the station, serious, frowning. They have separated Ursula and me for questioning. The lights are blinding and everything looks linoleum, even his eyes.

"I was on my way for frozen yogurt."

"And your friend?"

"She ran. She was in shock."

"I advise you to get a new friend." I smile but I realize the cop is not joking.

He has me flip through hundreds of headshots, endless faces laminated and organized in a three-ring binder. I close my eyes to focus but I can only recall his low, gruff voice, the nob of gun in my side. The officer asks if the gun was real, but how am I to know?

"I'm sorry." I realize I am apologizing a lot today. "I don't think I can identify him."

"We'll keep looking," he insists. "Maybe a photo will spark your memory."

When I get to the end of the binder, there is another binder. After the third, he lets me go. Urs is waiting for me. We decide we definitely deserve some frozen yogurt now. We take the subway one stop and fill our cups way over their tops.

"Fuck that cop," I say. "I don't want a new friend. I want you."

I'm crying again when I go to 77th Street to see Corey that night. "You need to be more careful," he says, and takes me up into the big, warm space of his chest.

"I think you should see someone your age," he tells me the next morning. His chin is scratchy, his eyes sad. I think of the boys in my Literature Humanities class, their earnestness.

"I like seeing you."

But Corey is gone. He doesn't answer his phone, his door. We don't have a world in common, friends, a life. I write him a letter, and leave it shoved under his apartment door.

I try a poem.

Like the lobster pot, I think. I cry a lot.

I admire you, beloved, for the trap you've set. It's like a final chapter no one reads because the plot is over, O'Hara writes.

When I visit my parents in Hoboken, I see his father's restaurant has closed its doors. The gelato cart is gone. A tanning parlor has opened in its place. The orange awning is grayish. Winter comes, New York gets cold and the cold cuts through my bones, sharp and stinging and wild.

Azeitão

The cool girls are different in college. They go to parties far, far away in Brooklyn and come back with paint streaked across their backs. They are always eating wonderful things. Cornbread muffins, JJ's curly fries, roti rolls stuffed with eggplant and paneer from Bombay Frankie. Fancy sandwiches on crusty baguettes. Many beers and bottles of Two Buck Chuck. And always they are skinny.

Urs is a cool girl, skinny, although she gets me. We never talk about the weight I am losing, my fear and obsession of food. When I can't sleep, I knock on her door. She is always up.

"Do you want some?" She offers me some chewy ginger candies. They look like bliss.

"No thanks." No way am I eating candy these days. She pops one in her mouth. I can smell the sharp sweetness. We sit on the floor together, our backs against her bed.

"I told you I was anorexic in middle school, right?" She may have mentioned it. I want to hear more, but I don't want to pry. I don't want to have to talk about my own shit.

"I think so."

"It got really bad. My hair fell out in clumps. I ended up in the hospital."

"Oh my god. I'm so sorry."

"It's okay. I'm better now. I think going through that made me really love food."

"What happened? How did you get healthy?"

"Well, the doctor told me to eat a lot of bananas and avocados." I think, *Maybe I'm eating too many bananas and they're making me fat.*

"So you just started eating bananas and avocados and everything got better?" I ask.

"It wasn't so much the bananas and avocados," she admits. "I was so exhausted from not eating. I was too tired to starve myself anymore. And I didn't want to die."

I want to hear more, but I don't want to reveal what I am doing to myself. I wonder if she knows. I am jealous of Urs's flat stomach, her compact breasts. She doesn't need to wear a bra. I wish I could wear her halter tops, her backless dresses. I wonder how miraculous my life would be in her body.

"You know," she says, "being skinny is such a strange part of beauty. It's not the most important part. It's just the only part you can control."

It's as if she can read my mind.

I tell her about Corey, a million times over, and she listens. We share clothes sometimes. She has decided to double major in music and biology, and she is always stressed, up all night studying. I still don't know what I will choose for a major. We eat grapefruits on her dorm room floor, pulling apart their segments. Grapefruits I can eat. They spray citrus perfume into the cold air and I can pick and pick on their generous flesh for only a hundred calories.

At midnight, I tell her good night. She laces up her sneakers and goes to the gym. (I work out in the morning, before I can do anything else. By night, I am spent.) Campus crawls with nighttime studiers, lovers. Without Corey's stories, my head's chatter is wild. I write poems again, moving the cursor forward on the screen with words words words. I have new time without Corey. I think, *I should get a job.*

I'm still a freshman and hungry when I get hired at Picholine, the fanciest of fancy restaurants on Manhattan's Upper West Side. I'm dazzled by the chandeliers, the intricacy of their baubles, the plush rugs that are infinitely more comfortable to sprawl on than my dorm room's twin bed.

I'd discovered the position on Craigslist during an insomnia-induced search, and deliberated carefully. It is the un–gelato shop: an esteemed Michelin-starred fine dining French place by Lincoln Center with grand chandeliers and plush forest-green tapestries on the walls. They are known for pioneering serious cheese in NYC—they have a beloved cheese cart. And an almost-celebrity chef, blond and pixelated in the newspaper, grinning over a plate of something meticulous. I can think of nothing more riveting. And so I send my résumé.

I credit my new skinniness with helping land me my job at The Piche.

I bought a black dress from Loehmann's in a smaller-than-ever size for the interview. "You look so fancy," a man in an artfully askew cap told me on the subway.

"You go to Columbia?" the GM asks during my interview. He has an expensive suit, a poochy belly, and a frown.

I have no experience. I am hired on the spot.

It is the sparkliness of my fantasies, realized. Skinny girls in unfathomably skinny dresses. Silver trays full of tall glasses of champagne. Sumptuous velvet curtains flank the door. At The Piche, backwaiters pull out chairs before you think to sit, fold your napkin into an elaborate sculpture while you're in the bathroom. Everything shines. Everything is just so. Everything is gorgeous.

The interview took place in the back office. It is a different planet than the dining room: fluorescent lights, prodigious piles of papers, many people wheeling about on big chairs in a miniature space. The dining room is the stage; back here is where the actors muster their poise, down coffee, snack on chewy bread butts, exchange mean gossip, filthy jokes, and laugh until their ribs hurt.

"This is a fancy restaurant. You will make the first impression. You should look put together, pretty, and, most of all, never skanky." The GM doesn't say the word *skanky*, I don't think, but such is his message.

This is what it takes to work in this New York institution: smile, be skinny, and have an Ivy League education, even just one semester.

I break into a smile on Broadway, traffic whizzing around me. This job feels important, the start of something grand.

Yet I feel a fraud. I am not how I appear. It is only time before they see through me, before I feast like my stomach wants, my heart wants, and my thighs swell in my tiny pants, stretching and stretching, ripping the seams. They cannot contain me for long. Of this, I am sure.

As a hostess, I am forbidden from cracking my knuckles or smoothing my hair in the dining room, which turns out to be more of a challenge than I had realized. I never know what to do with my hands. "Stand up straight," the maître d' hisses, and only then do I realize I'm leaning on the shiny wood of the host stand. On Tuesdays, Wednesdays, Thursdays, the occasional Friday, I take the 1 train downtown to Lincoln Center after class and change into my black pumps, the black blazer I leave in the coatroom that smells of overripe cheese and Febreze.

At preshift meetings, we gather around table 44 to swirl gewürztraminer over starched linens, stick our noses deep into glasses, discuss. "Rose petals," a server says, his tie inhumanly perfect. "The first ones that fall, from a lush garden in high summer."

"Lychee and honeycomb."

"Pumpkin seeds, roasting in a hot, hot oven."

"A Bartlett pear, not quite ripe, but getting there."

I don't know what to say, or what exactly I smell in the designer wine glass in front of me, but I feel giddy. The manic energy and knife-sharp focus, the boxes of heady truffles and sunshine-colored kumquats, the excruciatingly late nights, fur coats, basement arguments, VIPs, rabbit risotto, twinkly eyes. I've found my people, my place. It's everything I thought it would be, reading *Kitchen Confidential* behind the gelato cart. When I get back to my dorm room after my shift, the buzz still surges through my veins.

I'd give anything for a heaping bowl of the signature rabbit risotto, a whole loaf of the cranberry-hazelnut bread the backwaiters cut to order for cheese service, slathered in butter and sprinkled with sea salt. I am so hungry my stomach is perpetually achy and the room sometimes breaks into dots, as if the world is an impressionist painting. I am in love with this place that feeds people fantasy—panna cotta light as the puffiest cloud, foie gras smooth as silk, plates made exact with tweezers, cities built of matchsticks of veggies, everything is so perfect it hurts.

At The Piche, we sell a pretty story. Luxury. Rich butternut squash and duck flecked with white truffle, warm Maine lobster with caramelized endive and vanilla brown butter, venison with parsnip toast and huckleberries. Old-school New York. Jacket required. Perfection at $112 for four courses.

My job is to be like the chandeliers, all endless glass baubles reflecting light into dazzling prisms. Unreal.

"Hostesses are the trophy wives of the restaurant biz," my coworker tells me. "The point is to be fuckable."

Jehona, a tiny girl from Albania, oversees my induction into the world of hostessing. Her accent is thick, her ring huge, her demeanor a dizzying, seesawing affair of lighthearted and serious, giggly and furious.

"Don't mess with Albanians," Jose, the Mexican backwaiter, tells me by way of warning. But I don't need warning, I can see it in her eyes.

Us hostesses, we are quite a crew. There is an opera singer who practices in the coat closet before service, her soprano floating past the kitchen and onto 66th Street. Laura has a Southern drawl and has just moved to New York to become a model. She is skinnier than me, her anorexia more obvious. We ride the 1 train home together, sometimes uptown. She is fired for smoking pot before service with a blond cook. (The cook is not fired.) The Albanian girls wear a lot of makeup and are always watching their figures, which seems to me a retro thing to say.

Mateo, the single male host, is tall, handsome, Spanish, and has just graduated from hotel school in Europe. He wears a shiny suit and a slim tie. We flirt until he shows me pictures of his fiancée in Japan, his arms wrapped around her tiny waist, both of them looking away from the camera.

It is Jehona who takes me under her wing. She is stern. Also, she cares. She tells me stories of her apartment in Queens, which she shares with her fiancé's parents and many siblings. There are loud fights and silent ones. Work here is a kind of blessed escape.

In time, I'm sure I would have gathered that although family meal was often a dismal affair, the bountifully pierced, do-ragged pastry cook was generous with his chocolate soufflés—they rose in lofty splendor—and his petit fours. I would have learned on my own that Jason, one of the cheese guys, liked to share his craft with cheese-loving employees. But learning these things from Jehona, who gave her nuggets of knowledge like gifts, was sweeter than piecing it together by myself.

"Would you like some of this?" she says of her half-eaten soufflé. "I'm watching my figure." I'm watching my figure, too, like an enemy. Watching it and willing it to shrink, seeing everything but myself in the mirror. The battle rages on, makes my eyes ache deep in my skull, but I am too ashamed to speak of it.

We stash our food in the coat closet. Above the furs and backup jackets for the male guests who neglect to show up wearing their own, there's a little shelf where we leave plates of cheese and membrillo, the staff meal we didn't have time to eat.

Eventually I would have figured out that it was the unofficial duty of the hostess to double as sports announcer. Between walking aging hedge fund guys and tourists to their tables and directing guests toward the restrooms—with an outstretched palm, never point—I am expected to deliver regular updates on football and baseball scores to the guys on the floor and in the kitchen. I am bad at sports and numbers, so I take notes on the back of soignés, slips we hand to the kitchen for VIPs. They say *Mrs. B likes soft cheeses only* or *Do not ask about the doctor's wife under any circumstances.* On the back—*Mets 4, Royals 7.* The sous chef nods solemnly as I deliver both pieces of news.

Jehona's advice is occasionally invaluable. The maître d' might not be our official boss, she informs me, but he wields tremendous power. It is he who would decide my fate—both whether I get to keep my job and how joyful or miserable my time at The Piche will be.

If the maître d' flings rubber bands at your back when nobody is looking, it means he likes you.

The job is in no way challenging. During a pre- or post-theater rush or a whirring Saturday night, there is the need to keep calm, professional, centered in the midst of organized chaos. But the big decisions are left in the hands of the maître d'. His job is a different story.

He decides who sits at table 47, which is the best table, in the corner, and who gets 32, which is a cramped, ad hoc affair pushed between two nicer tables, and only when The Piche is buzzing. The flow of the night belongs to him. Regulars shake his hand with two of theirs, ask about his family who he never mentions to us.

Our job: look pretty. Be nice. Let the chef know that Mr. Brumnose is allergic to shellfish. Don't lean on the host stand. Stand up straight. Say "Good night, Mrs. Pinter, we hope to see you soon."

One day, I catch the opera-singing hostess and the GM slinking out of the coatroom together. They say it's the only nook of the restaurant without cameras. There's a velvety white wrap that sits on the back shelf for weeks. "Do you think I can snag it?" I ask Jehona. It's clearly neglected.

"It would look beautiful on you," she says, and saunters off in her heels. I wear it all winter and into spring.

When I am not walking regulars and B-list celebrities to table 12, or 39, or 47, I get up close and personal with the famous cheese cart, where I learn about Alpine wonders, buttery robiolas, washed-rind stinkers and the brilliant monks who coax them into perfection. "Holy shit," Max, the cheese man, says, deadpan. "The Constant Bliss is bliss right now." He holds it up to the light.

Here, a decade ago in 1995, Max started the country's first serious cheese program. After years of walking through the Upper West Side Michelin-starred fine dining establishment, back and forth and back and forth with his masterpiece—sometimes nearly a hundred cheeses from milk of Oregon cows and French mountain sheep elegantly assembled each night on a wooden cart—his eyes still light up as he tastes a piece of Berkswell. Mine light up, too.

There's something about cheese that wins my heart, immediately and entirely. The funk, the stink, the sweet. Cheese possesses magic powers. Cheese makes people happy. Cheesy days win over cheeseless days, every time. Cheese is a living, breathing food that coagulates, ferments, molds, breathes, ages, oozes, and sings.

On any given night the cart houses crumbly blues; soupy, stinky, washed-rind cheeses that have to be placed in a bowl and scooped out with a spoon; Max's "Swiss army" of Alpines; spicy cheddars; fresh goat cheeses wrapped in little packages with chestnut leaves and tied with twine. "This is good," he says. "Try this." And if Max says it's good, it's probably better than good. The Berkswell is sweet and nutty and my eyes water with shame and delight.

Hostesses can sit in on the preservice meetings, if we want, and I always want. We discuss kumquats and uni and sunchokes, rabbit risotto and sabayon. We swirl wine and pop champagne and take notes. My mind explodes. In this chandeliered restaurant with a coat closet full of furs, I feel alive.

I try a bite of Portuguese *azeitão*. (Do you know this cheese? You should know it. It is sheepy, feety, savory, and revelatory.) There are fireworks. But then I worry about my new size-tiny jacket and resolve to eat nothing else that day. It is worse than worry, a savage fear that makes my stomach sourer than azeitão.

I am fascinated by the emergence of my own pointy hipbones, the concave scoop above my clavicle. I keep fingering my shoulder, where I can make out the indentations of muscles and bones I never knew I had before. The pain in my butt changes from a dull ache to a sharp throb, which both impresses and scares me. I know this new body is unreal. It does not belong to me. I haven't gotten my period in months. I pass out in Pilates class, which I go to every morning, pumping my arms until they feel not like arms but like angry ghosts. I daydream about soft-ripened cheeses.

"What are you doing tonight?" I ask my new college friends. Even with my new job, the space Corey has left in his absence is cavernous. In the daytime, my life without him sometimes seems an adventure, like I'm spelunking, bopping around with fancy headgear into new crevices of my collegiate life. I go to my favorite professor's office hours. He wears elbow patches on his ill-fitting blazer like a professor from a movie and inserts so many classical references into every conversation I know what he means maybe half the time. We sit around drinking peppermint tea and talking about his future book. "Don't steal my ideas," he asks of me, and I feel flattered. With my classmates, I subway down to the Cornelia Street café to watch him read his poems, snap with them in appreciation. We loll around, when it's warm, on the lawn or the steps to Butler Library, reading and not reading, trying to impress each other and not trying at all.

"I thought you were a snob," one of them tells me. "But now I know better."

Nighttime, the lonely cave turns deeply scary. Alone, my dorm room's walls shrink around me. I try to get some reading done for class, there's always endless reading that I should be doing for class, but I lose focus and read the same page twice and then three times. There is silvery laughter coming from the halls, which makes my loneliness sting worse. I think I hear bats, their long wings rustling. Or is it the scratching of my own brain?

So I leave my room to go where the almost friends go, to Pinnacle for pizza with ziti on top at midnight, or even later. The lights are neon inside, so that everyone looks slightly green. Outside on Broadway, New York winks, always full of promise at such a grand scale, I feel dizzy, hopeful. I guzzle Diet Coke and watch them eat. Sometimes Urs offers me a slice, but nobody says anything about my stubborn refusal. I nurse my own cocktail of awe and shame and jealousy. "Jude's friend knows someone who lives in a big house with a fireplace. Wanna go make fireplace s'mores?"

A house with a fireplace! I didn't know there were houses with fireplaces at Columbia. I had been to a frat party in one of the grand, decrepit old houses on 114th Street during the first week of college. Upon entering, the nostril-filling reek of old and less-old beer turned my stomach. There was orange soda–colored punch that I sipped at, afraid of the calories. Hungry, the alcohol rushed into me, fast, a flood of warm and woozy and eye-popping sugar. A pretty girl in a tube top and a pierced belly screamed at a frat boy with a smirk, "Where's my coat? You asshole! You stole my coat." Another pretty girl barfed in the corner. That was my first and last frat party.

So I reel a bit when we head back to 114th Street, frat row. But I'm with Ursula and Jude, who would never willingly venture into Greek territory. It's a foreign, grotesque land of popped collars, brutal hazing, and date rape. (Never leave your drink for a second lest it be roofied. Better yet, stay as far away as possible.)

The house looks like a frat house on acid. A skull and crossbones hangs outside on a droopy flagpole, billowing, the expansive flag grayed from city smog. Windy stairs curl up past a pool table, faded and saggy. (Later I learn that having sex on the pool table earns ironic bragging rights, which I fail to garner.) There are pictures of old, important men on the walls in ornate frames, but also a wall of mouths painted in watercolor and collages from magazine clippings in various states of decay. "Members Only," a sign says, but we head in anyway.

One of those chest-tall plastic dudes, the kind that offer up mints in cheesy Italian restaurants, perches by the entrance, his arms out-stretched. In the chipped bowl, a headless Barbie rises from a sea of condoms. "Take One, Please!" the cursive font reads.

By the fire, everyone is laughing, toasting marshmallows on sticks and drinking from real martini glasses, a sight strikingly elegant in college (in contrast: frat party Solo cups or the clear plastic numbers at the gallery openings and poetry readings we stalk just for the free vinegary wine). Sometimes we crash the business school parties for their superior snacks, cubes of pepper-flecked cheese, finger-sized pigs in blankets.

Here, bona fide glassware, triangular slopes making martini smiles. Olives. Twists. People smoke long cigarettes. Bookshelves line the walls, full of volumes of things. At the bar, which is an actual bar, a gray-eyed boy in a feathered cap makes me a martini. "It's free for pledges," he says, and kisses my hand. Maybe he's making fun of me, but his smile contains warmth I'm ravenous for, as do these walls, the crackle of the fire. Jude and Ursula are talking to girls in swirly dresses with bare feet. Someone has cracked the door to the fire escape. For the first time on this campus, I feel a little bit at home.

So I come back. I learn it's the non-frat fraternity, a coed "literary society" for artists and crossdressers and cokeheads and disaffected daughters of socialites who want to rebel. I want in, and so I become a pledge.

There are seven of us pledges, including a French exchange student who is curious about Greek culture even though we tell her this isn't exactly Greek culture from the movies. She is smart enough to get it and so are we. Pledge activities include a trip to Chinatown for soup dumplings, a ride on the tram to Roosevelt Island for no apparent reason, and a picnic beside Grant's tomb. We learn about the history of Samuel Eells, who founded the society in 1832. The haus (for some mysterious, pretentious reason, we call it the haus) puts on a big party and we help by selling tickets and pouring cheap champagne into plastic champagne glasses.

"I can help," I offer to our pledge mistress, Jodi. "But I'll be a little late. I'll come straight after work."

Jodi takes her position literally, always wearing dominatrixesque boots and plenty of leather.

"That's fine," she says.

When I get to the haus, it is full of smoke from cigarettes and weed, teenage bodies pressed together, high heels kicked off in corners, music so loud my body purrs with it.

Jodi tells me I can change in her room, but there are five guys in suits sitting around chatting. They have Eastern European accents; they look much older than us.

"Excuse me," I tell them. "I didn't know you'd be in here."

"Hi! We're friends of Jodi."

"Cool, me too."

I change in the bathroom, out of my black Piche suit and into a dress smaller than anything I would have had the courage to wear prediet. There are two people making out, or maybe more than making out, in the stall next to me. I dance with Jude. I dance with my pledge brother Dan and my new friend Taylor. I dance with Jodi and her graduate school boyfriend. I dance with the Eastern Europeans, who turn out to be Albanians like Jehona. I am so tired and hungry I feel like I may turn to pixie dust and float out onto the fire escape, into the city sky. We fall asleep in Jodi's room, in a cloud of marijuana and music and euphoria.

On a Tuesday, I wake up to a letter shoved under my dorm room door. I have been admitted to the society. I have to show up at night to accept. I put on a sweater and head out to the steps outside of Low Library. For once, they are empty. It is spring but Christmas lights still twinkle on trees. Jodi gives me a hug. Dan looks high out of his mind and happy. We huddle together, all seven of us, campus stretched around us, New York City beyond that. I think, *This is what I wanted.* This is everything I want. To be part of a group that's not just any group. A group where I want to belong. A group where I do.

Because I don't believe I am likable, even for a second, attention from men surprises me, every time. When a cute cook named Damien asks me out, I think he is making fun of me. Damien has a goofy smile and a lot of energy. All the cooks say "Oui, chef" like a chorus, but Damien says it loudest. He sometimes brings me a candied kumquat to try when there is a slow moment, a spoonful of horseradish foam on a paper-thin slice of rib eye.

"You like burgers, right?"

"Of course." Who doesn't like burgers? I never eat burgers, but I want to sound easygoing.

"What's your favorite burger?"

I don't know. Growing up without much red meat and spending the last almost year on a perpetual diet, I can't remember a burger gracing my lips.

"The Spotted Pig, totally." I read the food blogs, and I've ogled pictures of the famous chargrilled patty, blanketed with a sea of Roquefort. It's a half lie.

After work, we go for burgers at Island Burgers and Shakes, piled high with avocado and melty cheddar. I cannot remember the last time I ate an actual burger. The level of goodness is impossible. I try to make myself throw up in the bathroom, but the food is stuck in my chest. We go for a walk after dinner, and I feel the burger dispersing into my body, as if it's flowing into the soft spot of my stomach, the outside of my thighs, staying there forever.

Damien kisses me at Columbus Circle. It is 2 AM and the fountain is glistening just for us, majestic. Fifty-Ninth Street is quiet. For a minute, I think I feel what it must be like to be pretty, chosen.

The next week, he meets me at Otto. It's his day off. We sit at the bar and order wine and charcuterie, translucent slices of pork streaked with pearly fat. He excuses himself to go to the bathroom. I swing my legs from the tall barstool, the fat dissolving on my tongue. Minutes pass, then more minutes.

I think he must have made a break for it, but his puffy coat still hangs on the back of his barstool, his wine glass nearly full.

"Need anything?" the bartender wants to know.

"I don't know! My date went to the bathroom . . . fifteen minutes ago? More?"

"Hmm," he says, and tops me off. More minutes pass. I try not to finish my wine.

The guy next to me has been listening. "I'll go check on him," he says. "I'm a doctor. It's been more than twenty minutes, I think. What's his name?"

"Damien."

When the doctor returns, he is alone. "Damien has low blood sugar. Dangerously low. I've called 911. Did you know he was diabetic?"

"I didn't know."

The bartender fills a glass with orange juice.

I feel helpless, don't know what to do. I think about passing out in Pilates class, the embarrassment of waking up to the teacher over me. I think about how fragile our bodies are. I think about what I am doing to mine.

Two paramedics arrive, burly and brusque, hold Damien up by the armpits as he heads out to an ambulance, blinking its lights down 8th Street into the setting sun. Damien's face looks waxen.

"Do you want me to come with you?" I ask him. I want to be useful.

"No, no, no."

I ask the paramedics if I should come, anyway, if he needs someone with him.

"The man said no."

I text and call and text again. No word. He's at work the next day, but won't answer when I ask him what happened, if he's okay.

"I'm here, aren't I?"

I keep checking my phone until it buzzes with: *I can't hang out anymore. Please understand.*

I am learning so many things at The Piche: that good consommé is translucent as glass, that squab is a fancy word for pigeon, that there are endless varieties of caviar. The lady always gets the banquette, and the table should be pulled out in one swift motion to let her in without squatting. Finished oysters are discarded craggy shell side down. Damien goes back to picking leaves of chervil. I stand at the pass for a second, stealing a glimpse of him picking, chopping, laughing. "Oui, chef!" he calls. I feel wobbly, like I need all the glasses of orange juice in the world, a sea of sugary tenderness.

When the astral-eyed Executive Chef invites me for drinks, I say yes, too. All the hostesses have a crush on him. His face appears on the newsstands, his glossy smile, a "best new chef." Here, he may as well be George Clooney. Part of me knows it is a mistake, a joke that he has picked me and not one of the models. I am waiting for him to crack up in laughter, but he never does.

I wait for him outside after work. Lincoln Center is aglow in drizzly mist. I think, *This is what I wanted.* I'm skinny and eighteen and about to go out with a Michelin-starred, kind-of celebrity chef. I wonder why I'm not elated.

"You're beautiful," he tells me. The claim sounds ridiculous, cruel. "I don't think so."

"What? How can you not think so?" And I see I have fooled him, too. "I'm glad it is raining so we have to share an umbrella." It is one of the restaurant's umbrellas that he has snagged from the coat closet, and under its green plastic arms he kisses me with wet, impatient lips. I don't particularly want him, but being wanted makes up for it. Raindrops are drumbeats above us.

The bar at our sister fancy restaurant down the street is nearly empty. We drink wine more expensive than anything I own. When our glasses are empty, he gets a cab to his place. I don't think about protesting, although my forehead is sweaty with fear. At his Upper East Side apartment, all window and wood, he pours us more wine, plays jazz. He kisses me hard, cups just my left breast, pulls out his dick, but it is as soft as his famous soufflé. Drunk, we fall asleep on his white leather couch.

I wake up so panicked I have to hold my hand over my heart to feel its faint thump. My skin sticks to the couch. He is slumped over, snoring faintly. I am still here, alive, queasy. My hangover hurts. Yesterday, I "ate" only coffee, yogurt, and too much wine. I leave without saying goodbye, buy a seltzer from the bodega on the corner, ask the guy behind the counter which way to the subway.

When I get back to campus, I text Urs from my dorm room. We go to the dining hall, which we usually avoid; the food is terrible. But

I'm hungover and tender and I can't fight my body's animal urge to eat today. I load my tray with greasy eggs and little blueberry muffins and spongy French toast. I tell her about the chef and she tells me about her violinist ex-girlfriend who won't stop calling. I wonder if it's easier or harder to date both men and women—twice the opportunity for love and twice the opportunity for heartbreak.

The food tastes wonderful and gross. After, we fill our bags with dining hall bananas and apples and yogurts to bring back to our dorms. It's only half stealing.

At work the next night, Chef averts his eyes when our paths cross. I have to take a break to cry in the bathroom. I wonder if he has rejected me because I am getting fatter, fat. I wish I could take back that dining hall meal. At The Piche, the light is so exquisitely dim, I can't tell if my eyeliner has run down my face with my tears, but Damien asks if I am okay.

I am not okay.

I am so hungry.

Love, dread. The foie gras, the caviar, the chandelier, the fresh flowers taller than I am, the love, the sex. I am eighteen and this is it, all there is, my enemies, my salvation.

"This way, please," I say, stifling any residual sniffles, walking the suits to table 52, pulling out a sleek chair.

Springtime chirps its birdsounds. My freshman year is coming to its end. After our last finals but before we leave for summer, the senior who led our COHOP trip invites Urs and me to see his art show in Bushwick. We ride the L train for ages. The sky is wet and dark, and we wear each other's dresses, sling our arms over each other's shoulders on Flushing Ave. Murals make the low, boxy buildings seem alive. The streets are nearly empty.

The warehouse is cavernous. The gallery is filled with giant wooden sculptures—naked beams with splintered edges, like deformed treehouses. Between the broken treehouses, a naked man with matted hair grown so long it reaches his butt is yodeling—performance art. "Stop giggling," Urs has to tell me. We drink brackish white wine from plastic cups. Downstairs there is a band, a sea of hands thrust skyward. It smells of sweat and impending rain. We find our friend.

"Your art is amazing," we scream over belly-thrumming bass. "Thanks for inviting us."

"The *New York Times* is here, and they like it!" He's so happy, his voice sounds like the yodeling upstairs, buoyant.

"I'm so happy for you! Congrats!"

He gets all serious. He is older and wiser and about to graduate and head off into the thicket of the real world. He's also the guy who led us in eating games in the Adirondacks, built a fire to burn the remains of our half-cooked beans, bellowed like a wolf as we descended the mountain.

"Hey, listen." His voice drops. The band is taking a break and the party quiets to the dull vibration of crowd sound.

"We all got into Columbia because we're good at doing what we're supposed to do. Acing the test. Jumping through the hoops. But sometimes it's better to say fuck the tests, fuck the hoops, fuck what we're supposed to do. Anyway. Have fun. Follow your heart. And all that shit. Just because it looks shiny doesn't mean you have to do it. I wish someone told me that when I was eighteen."

"So what are you going to do after graduation?"

"Travel the world. Make art."

I've spent so much time trying to do everything right, to succeed. But why? *Travel the world. Make art.* It sounds like a recipe for joy.

The party is reaching a frenzy, bodies pressing up against each other into a mass of energy.

"Want to get out of here?" I ask.

"My ears hurt," Urs agrees.

Outside, the Brooklyn sky feels unfathomably big. It's started to rain, slow, fat drops that plop on my head, my nose.

"Are you hungry?" Urs asks.

I'm always hungry. On the way home, we stop at Big Nick's on 71st Street, running from the subway, thundering skies, puddles already pooling on Broadway. The booth's worn leather squishes beneath my butt. These days, it always hurts a little to sit. Big Nick's has a menu thick as a bible, which lists every dish, conceivable or not. There are bison burgers, salmon burgers, tuna, turkey, veggie, bean burgers. Urs gets a classic cheeseburger. I flip through the pages, deliberate over what I won't hate myself worse in the morning for ordering. I choose mushroom barley soup, which tastes vaguely of swimming pool.

"Want a bite of my burger?" she offers, but I refuse. I know I can't stop at a bite. I try to read her. She must know I am barely eating. Is she pissed? She seems only vaguely concerned.

"Are you sure? It's really good. You could have just a small bite." But I change the subject. I am not ready to talk to anyone about what I do and don't do with food. I am barely ready to admit it to myself. What's wrong with mushroom barley soup?

We're getting sentimental—the last day of the first year, a summer stretched out before us.

"Can we make a pit stop before we go home?" I ask.

Our dresses are dripping rain by the time we make it to 77th and West End, Corey's apartment building, puddles at our feet and in our hair. Steep steps, handsome brownstone. I wonder if he's sitting now inside on his lumpy couch beside a girl with big eyes and slender fingers. Or maybe he has moved to Florida and is standing under a palm tree, his strong back against its trunk. Or maybe he is sitting in traffic, late for work.

"What do you want to do?"

"It feels symbolic. The storm is going to wash away the last of this. I don't want to think about Corey anymore."

"Hell yeah," Urs agrees, and we stand in silence, the rain pattering and swirling in the wind, before we get a cab up to 115th Street.

Summer sighs its swampy air. I pack up my red blanket, my towers of books, give Urs a series of teary hugs. In Hoboken, the air conditioning paints everything in chill. I commute on the PATH train from my parents' Hoboken apartment to The Piche.

One afternoon, everyone is scrambling to finish what they are doing, mise-en-place in their places, tablecloths starched and ironed crisp as autumn. I am running from the office to the host stand with the night's seating charts, VIPs and Chef's aunt are coming in, there is an engagement party in the PDR (that's private dining room) . . . and there is Damien, on the floor in the fluorescent-lit hallway outside the kitchen, legs pushed up into his chest.

"Are you okay?"

"Can you bring me some OJ from the bar?"

I fill a quart container with the pulpy stuff and he cups it in his shaky hands. I cross my legs, join him on the linoleum.

For a while, we just sit, a bubble of quiet in the hustle.

"All right, Hannah, I got this. You can go back to work." And so I do.

Hours later, in the middle of service, I pop my head in the hot kitchen. In his station on the line sits a sparkly cutting board, clean nine pans heaped with green garlic and red cabbage confit, but no Damien.

"What happened?" I ask Jehona, who always seems to know everything.

"He went home sick," she says. Nobody goes home sick at The Piche. It's the restaurant code of honor. I think of the ambulance disappearing into traffic the other night. There is a couple at the door, and I take them to table 26.

Pastéis de Nata

After freshman year—which feels more like a decade than like nine months of walking ballet dancers and hedge fund big shots to their tables again and again; reading *The Peloponnesian Wars*, reading *To the Lighthouse*; getting lost in Bed-Stuy at night after someone's party, which turns out to be a recruitment for some kind of new-age religious cult; buying fake designer jeans from the runner, Jose, in the alley by the dumpsters for twenty dollars; tasting summer Comté with Max, eating as little as I can manage—I decide to take a break from my shifts at The Piche to go on a two-week trip to Portugal with two of my Baltimore friends, Steph and Amanda. We find cheap flights. It will be an adventure.

As soon as I get off the airplane in Lisbon, something feels off. Our hugs are perfunctory. Between the three of us, it is nothing like it was just a year ago, in Baltimore, the way just seeing their faces was home, the way their laughter turned on a switch of my own giggling that couldn't be stopped for hours, even if I tried to think of terribly serious matters. These were the non-ribbon-wearing girls, the smart girls, the interesting girls. These were the girls who understood me. I'm secretly excited for them to see my new body, my new life.

We do not have a fun time. We fight about directions to the hostel. We fight about whether to see an old castle or a sculpture museum or both or neither. We fight about where to go for dinner.

"You look really skinny," Steph says, only once. We're unpacking our toiletries in the hostel in Lisbon and her forehead scrunches in disapproval. "Like a different person."

"I'm still me," I tell her in defense. "I've been doing Pilates."

I wonder if she's jealous, but she seems only repelled, as if I've become hideous. I realize I want her approval, her eyes on me in the first bikini I have ever worn. It's as blue as the ocean past the cliffs of the Praia do Castelo. From the side, you can see the snake of my breast reduction scar peeking out from its slick fabric. I want her to see me. I want her love.

I want to tell her and Amanda about the strange worlds I've discovered, about Corey and the cheese cart and even about *To the Lighthouse*, but they seem uninterested or worse. They want to talk about silk scarves and messy roommates. These are the girls who stayed up all night with me after mixers to gossip about the cool girls, to map out the terrain of the rest of our lives. My weight seems the least of what has changed between us.

I eat, but I know I'm not eating like a normal person. I manage breakfast, lunch, and dinner, mostly, sort of, but when Steph and Amanda stop for afternoon ice cream, I shake my head no. We get three spoons with our raisin-and-cinnamon-covered rice pudding at the fancy food court at El Corte Inglés, but I only hold mine up to my mouth, metallic at my lip, as if I'm just about to dig in. I'm terrified of unleashing the monster for whom all the lacquered candies and fluffy pastries at El Corte Inglés are nowhere near enough. I'm afraid of putting on that bikini tomorrow, which seemed like a good idea for a moment—the woman in the dressing room next to me told me it was beautiful, even with my scars showing. But now it feels like a cruel joke I played on myself. In the hostel mirror, my thighs pucker and ooze.

I'm obsessed with saving the miniscule calories I allot myself for the very best food Portugal has to offer—no mediocre street ice cream or chips from bags, only grilled sardines that taste of charred sea, juicy chicken fiery with *piri piri*, fatty, sour sheep's milk cheeses, the grapefruit effervescence of vinho verde. But Steph and Amanda don't want to go to the restaurants I've meticulously researched, and I'm tired of fighting with them. One day at the beach, the sky beginning to blush with dusk, I read a book alone while they splash in the waves. I take a walk, toes sinking into the wet smooth of the sand, as they head back to the hostel to shower, their melodious voices receding over the sand dunes. The Atlantic rushes up to my ankles, the beach smells of wind and sardines. My loneliness feels as wide as its endless expanse.

Finally, we all agree that we want to try *pastéis de nata*, the little Portuguese egg custard tarts in crackly, buttery pastry. We trek to the place we hear is best, a long walk in the midday sun to a charm-filled café with cerulean tiles on the ceiling, no-joke espresso, guitar on the radio. We order a half dozen for us to share. I want to try them, but I can't. I just can't. The espresso is bitter and black. Steph and Amanda's conversation may as well be in Portuguese.

I examine the custard, yellow as sunflowers, the gilded glow of the pastry that surrounds it. I watch them eat.

"You're not going to have any, are you?" Amanda accuses, and I take a small bite to prove her wrong. Butter, egg, and sugar. It's explosive in its wonderfulness, it's too much, too generous, still warm, richer than my sadness, almost.

"They're delicious," I tell Amanda and Steph, but they're only looking at each other.

I want to eat the pastéis de nata and I don't want to eat the pastéis de nata. I am trapped. Either way, I will let myself down. How is a small plate of pastries so much bigger than me?

After Portugal, I go back to work at The Piche for the rest of the summer. The PATH train is so hot that I feel my skin liquefying, my blood turning to steam. I stop wearing makeup, which only melts.

I set out to work in food because I can't see another way. Food has my heart. Onions caramelizing, the sizzle of sweet alchemy, the whole home warm with happy fragrance. Dipping a crusty piece of sourdough into gold-green olive oil, the oil's sting on the back of my throat. The tiniest bubbles of champagne.

I want to be as close to food as possible. I want to sprinkle snow-white pyramids of fresh chèvre with black ash. Flip a fat, red steak in a heavy pan, ladle bubbly butter on top of its flank, watch the steak drink it in and in.

I am a voyeur: I want to watch you eat it. The way your eyes widen, just a bit, the corners of your mouth tilt upward, an almost smile, a smile. The way you swipe the plate clean of the last drop of sauce with your bread, every bit of the good stuff.

I want the good stuff.

In the kitchen, that's where the magic happens.

I also know that women must be thin to be worthy, good. I am everything but—too tall, too wide, too much. Always have been, no matter what I do to protest and fight. My shoulders are broad. My boobs are huge, still, post-surgery, horrifyingly so. I fantasize about butchering myself the way the cooks I work with so beautifully break down a side of beef, carving away the excess until I'm okay. Their knives slice through fat smooth as butter.

The food, I could blissfully eat it until my stomach presses against my organs and each breath takes work. But I learn that I can eat less and less and make myself less and less.

Not eating makes me feel powerful, but my goal is never to starve. I am obsessed with food. I read the new food blogs, every article and recipe in *Gourmet* and all of the cookbooks stacked in the Picholine office. My goal is to be so thin that it's okay, necessary, that I eat. Once I get to some magical, impossible land of skinnydom, I will stop starving and start living. I remember Corey saying "Just lose some weight, then you can go back to loving food." Am I there yet? That place does not exist. I will never arrive.

One afternoon at work, I am going over the guest list with the maître d' and see a familiar name: Astor Guest, the soap opera star, my middle school classmate, queen of the cool girls. Eight o'clock reservation for three.

I tell the maître d'. I tell Jehona. Suddenly, I am back in middle school dance class, feeling monstrous and lame.

My Piche people surprise me. They have my back.

"Was she your friend?"

"Oh no. She was way too cool to be my friend."

"Don't worry. We all hate her for you. Does she live in New York?"

"She's at college at Duke, she must be visiting, or acting in something."

"Duke?"

"Duke."

"She clearly couldn't get into Columbia. She's definitely not as smart as you." All this from Jehona, who didn't go to college. I hug her right there in the dining room. When Astor comes in with her parents in pearls and khakis, she gives me the kind of hug where we don't really touch.

Her family opts out of the tasting menu and orders a few things à la carte—the butter-poached Maine lobster, the famous wild mushroom and rabbit risotto. Good choices, but when I walk past the table the food sits untouched. Astor's dad is playing with his phone. Her mom looks bored and so does she. After our not-hug hug, she ignores me, except for a noncommittal wave as Jehona hands the family their coats on their way out the door, holds out the sleeves so Astor's mom can duck into her silky jacket.

"It's been a long time since middle school," Jehona tells me in the coatroom. "You are prettier. You are nicer. And who wears khakis?"

The fabric of my black dress scratches around my shoulders, but I know it looks good. The maître d' waves down a cab for them, and as it slows on 64th Street I wonder why I spent so many years feeling inferior. Jehona has saved me a single chocolate truffle, on a tiny china plate on the corner shelf of the coat closet, above the shearlings and furs. I am a New Yorker. I am skinny. I have new friends in an old haus on 114th Street. Everything is just how I dreamed it may be, even better. Everything is going to be okay.

Night after night I watch the pastry cooks arrange layers of coconut and chocolate in geometry lessons of cubes and pyramids and globes, blow sugar shiny as jewels. Almost too pretty to eat. No matter how thin I get, it is not enough. I know what these people do not: at my core, I am a fat girl, and always will be. More than anything, my job is to make sure they don't find out.

I am trapped. I am here in this specter of Michelin stars, fresh flowers twice a week, sometimes three times, "may I take your coat, please" because I have fooled everyone. Seventeen days of so few calories, I have to steady myself when I get off the subway, lean against a pole, for a moment so wobbly I see myself careening down into the tracks. I know I may not make it until day eighteen. I can see the forthcoming binge. And then, my waist will expand like a balloon. I will be unfuckable, or even worse: unlikable, unacceptable, unlovable. The lie will pop, and they will fire me, and I will go back to being myself, lonely. I can imagine nothing more awful, and so I make it to day eighteen, nineteen, twenty. I am always exhausted and sleep is close to impossible. At night, I lie awake with Lacan, Derrida open on my bed.

I hate math, but I am always counting. Food is not just food but a vessel of points and calories, grams of carbs and fat. If I drink only coffee all day, I will allow myself dinner. If I don't eat dinner, I can eat an oatmeal raisin cookie. I bargain with myself. I am distracted in class. I care about poetry but I care more about that oatmeal raisin cookie. In my calendar, I jot down my weight each Thursday. I leaf through the pages to next month, next year. On which Thursday will I stop?

I know that it is not just my body that is fucked but my brain. The more weight I lose, the bigger I feel. I see a new problem, unsolvable. It is not that I am too fat, anymore, it is that my skeleton is too big. My rib cage seems a rib cage better suited for some kind of wild cat, not a human woman. How is it that I never noticed my rib cage before, its cumbersome circumference? My shoulders feel broader every day, my pelvis splayed to some ridiculous abyss of wideness.

My weird hours at The Piche mean I don't see my parents much, but on my day off my mom is home reading a book, drinking coffee. I realize it is Sunday. She offers me a cup and I accept.

"Steph's mom called."

"Oh?" My mom and Steph's mom used to be friends. They drank glasses of white wine while we played in Steph's tree-filled yard, called each other on the phone and didn't hang up for ages. But since we've moved to Hoboken, I didn't realize they still talked.

"Steph and Amanda were worried about you in Portugal. They told her that you weren't eating."

"I was eating! We had the most amazing octopus salad and these little tarts called pastéis de nata."

"They are worried about you."

"They didn't want to go to the restaurants I found."

"They told Steph's mom that you may have an eating disorder."

"They said that? To Steph's mom?" I am caught off guard by this betrayal. Why couldn't they have talked to me? My mom's eyes look heavy, as if she has been crying, but she only gives me a hug.

All this fucking with food started with the fierce urge to belong, but I feel more alone every day. Steph and Amanda don't say anything to me; I don't say anything to them.

"Do you think you have a problem?" Mom asks.

"I have more than one problem."

"Do you want to see someone?"

"No."

It's excruciating to discuss even in the vaguest terms. I'm the one who cries in my mom's arms. I wonder if she understands. I think of her own failed diets. Isn't this supposed to be what happens when diets work? Are Steph and Amanda just jealous? Aren't I a success story? Before and after?

The word *disorder* works. Eating dis-order. Things way far from harmony, embroiled in thick chaos. A chaos that doesn't just obscure truth, but ravages it to a messy pulp. I get to interview Daniel Boulud for a project and he invites me to a tasting menu at Daniel—ten courses with wine pairings—then fried chicken with my cook friends after they finish their shifts, the meat sweet on the bone, until I'm woozy with full, fat French fries, the giantest cup of fro-yo (more a bucket, really) with all the toppings on the way home, because I can't stop (the thought of doing so is not unnerving but unfathomable), a bowl of cereal, another one in bed, the crunch dry in my mouth as the sun creeps up, its light brilliant and bewildering.

And the next day, the debilitating nausea. The fierce resolution to never eat again, three days of two apples and a gazillion coffees. The spins. Sweat behind my knees and under my breasts. I touch my collarbones for evidence of my existence.

I'm too cool, of course, for this whole anorexia thing. Too smart. Eating disorders seem cheesy, predictable, fodder for after-school specials and teenage girls. Never mind that I am a teenage girl.

Also, I was in my mom's belly in 1986 in Washington, DC, at my first march for women's right to choose. I grew up hearing *a woman needs a man like a fish needs a bicycle,* and Gloria Steinem and Betty Friedan adorn my parents' bookshelves. I know the impossible bind of being valued for being sexy and condemned for being sexy. I know that my body is a source of both vulnerability and power and that navigating this is and will continue to be impossible. I want to be badass and free from the patriarchy. I want to be badass and free from the patriarchy *and* skinny.

I don't tell a soul about my eating disorder. When Urs shares her childhood bout with anorexia with me, it sounds like ancient history—passing out, hours of dance class, the way her bones seemed to go on and on forever. I think of my own middle school reflection in those dance class mirrors. I listen, fascinated, then change the subject. It is too close to home. I may give myself away. It doesn't occur to me that she knows, that everyone close to me knows.

Every Thursday, I weigh myself on the gym scale. If the number is smaller, I am triumphant and can have a good week, although sometime around Monday or Tuesday I start dreaming of the clunky balancing weights on the old-school scale going *ka-plunk, ka-plunk* until I've maxed out the scale with my hugeness. If the scale stays the same, it is proof I need to diet harder. I hunker down with my yogurts and my apples and my coffee. If the scale goes up, I have failed. I punish myself with extra time on the elliptical. When Urs asks if I want to grab dinner, I say I've already eaten.

The girl in the dorm room next door, a sophomore with cat's eye glasses and blonde curls down her back, knocks on my door to offer me a slice of pie she baked.

"Oh, thank you so much! That's so sweet of you. But I'm okay, I had a big dinner."

"Are you sure? It's really good. I hope that's not bragging."

"I'm sure."

"Hannah." She touches my shoulder. "You've lost a lot of weight." I shrug. "Let me know if you want to talk."

I don't want to talk. I am mortified. She leaves the pie anyway. It looks exquisite, with a crumbly crust blanketing apples and cranberries. I throw it in the trash, push it to the bottom of the bin with the paper plate.

I don't admit the depth of my despair to myself, even. I am just eating grapefruits for dinner so I can become a cool girl, so I can taste the freedom of a concave tummy and space between my thighs. Then I will spread peanut butter on sourdough with unbridled relish, share a plate of middle-of-the-night sweet potato fries, smile as I pass my reflection, float away in the ecstasy of skinny. I think of what Corey said: I can go back to loving food when I am thin enough.

I don't believe women, anyone, should be defined by how they look, the size of their upper arms. I check out someone's girlfriend on the subway, black hair and wild style and drop-dead curves. She is stunning. As I become skinnier, sicker, I look at people differently. I am jealous when I see skinny girls eating heartily. I wonder if they are going to throw up later. I wonder how they do it.

And yet. I think of how long I could go without eating—hours, days, maybe forever. I have that anorexic twist of the brain. Skinnier is better, always, when it comes to my own body, tall, unwieldy.

Even though I haven't gotten my period for months, I buy tampons at the drugstore, just in case, and the unopened boxes fill a whole drawer in my dorm room desk. I was so proud to be the first in my class to get my period, yet its absence feels like victory. I am winning. In class, I sit on my coat, my scarf, and it still isn't enough of a cushion. Still, I ache for skinnier. The promised land.

It doesn't stop and start with my body—cells and organs, blood and bones and limbs. Bathing suits, ice cream stands, size 2, size 0, mean boys, mean girls, family dinners, long nights alone, awake, sweaty sheets. But with my body, I can step on the scale and know its worth, quantify.

This obsession is the corporeal manifestation of my deepest fears and demons. So much joy that my rib cage threatens to shatter. It's a hiding place—armor, distraction. What longing.

I'm at the kitchen counter in Hoboken, home from school for a weekend. "I think you should see someone," my mom insists. The apartment smells of coffee and shampoo.

"I'm fine," I maintain but she doesn't believe me. I don't believe myself, either.

"Even so, it can't hurt to talk to a therapist."

Everyone has a therapist. Urs has a therapist. Jodi from the haus has a therapist. Why shouldn't I see one, too? Maybe she can help me be more relaxed about my diet. Maybe she can help me hate myself less. I relent.

I know something is wrong. The skinniness has not brought happiness. The Columbia mental health office only sees patients short term, so they refer me to a woman with long black hair and a long, flowy skirt. I walk down to 91st Street to see her on Thursdays. Urs's therapist is in the same building, so sometimes we schedule our appointments so we can go together, arm-in-arm down Central Park West. After, we stop for fro-yo.

When the therapist sends paperwork home—I use my parents' health insurance—there is the DSM code of an anorexia diagnosis, *anorexia nervosa*, spelled out in serious typeface. This time, my mom cries. It is official. My diet turned into anorexia. The anorexia feels like an awful joke.

It doesn't quite make sense to me. I wonder if my therapist has made a mistake. Do anorexics inhale whole trays of brownies, spend their work breaks huddled over shipments of sheep's milk ricotta?

"I don't think this is right," I tell my mom.

My mom has worked in the mental health world for her whole career. "She has to put something down on the insurance form," she says. "She's choosing the closest fit. I'm sorry," my mom tells me. "I thought you were doing something positive with this dieting. I shouldn't have encouraged it."

But it wasn't just her who encouraged it. It was the whole fucking world.

Hostessing bores me pretty quickly. Back and forth to table 23, 47, 52. Sports scores and confirming reservations. Mr. Ellsmore doesn't eat fish. Table 12 has a birthday. *Have a wonderful evening, we hope to see you again soon.* Hosts miss all the action, which happens in the kitchen, at the table.

I decide to talk to Max. After my reading for class, my papers on the "ethnography of the surreal," I read both of his books on cheese, flipping through glossy pages of speckled wheels and blue cheeses as green as the ocean and memorizing the best pairings for sheep's milk. I spend all the time I can at his cart, watching him spritz the orange Langres with champagne, carve a wheel of Appenzeller with wire. "I'm obsessed with cheese," I tell him before service one day. We're in the wine room—he's setting up his cart, I'm polishing wine glasses. "I want to learn everything. I know I have a lot more to learn, but I'm a good student. Would you consider training me for cheese service?"

"I'd love to!" he says enthusiastically. "Let me talk to the GM."

The GM calls me into his office the next day.

"You are unhappy with your job?"

"I'm not unhappy, just excited about cheese. I'd love to be able to contribute to The Piche in more ways and be able to help with cheese service. I love cheese so deeply. And Max is really busy."

"You don't need to worry about Max." He looks at me as if I am a naughty puppy.

"Even so. I know I can help with cheese service. What do you think?"

"You are a great hostess," he says. "We need you at the door."

The next week Mateo, the one male host among us, gets promoted. He will be working with cheese, learning from Max, they announce at our preshift meeting. Under the light of the chandelier, his suit gleams. He looks happy.

"Congratulations," I say, wondering if he can see straight through to my ire.

"I tried," Max tells me later that night. "There will be more cheese opportunity." I know he is right, but I am not good at patience.

This is a boys' club. There is a single woman cook in a sea of men. The only female server left for good on my second shift, her heels slung over her shoulder. I think, *Fuck that*. I think, *Fine, let Mateo have his cheese job*. I'm going to do something for real. I'm not going anywhere. I'm going to have my own restaurant, and it will be nothing like this. I'm not giving in.

I get an email that there is a room available at the haus, but I will have to share it with Jude. Summer before sophomore year, I move in. Jude takes the top bunk. My dad helps me carry my books, journals, red blanket, up the four flights of stairs to room 32.

Ursula laughs at me for being such a joiner—she's much too cool to be part of something like this—but she visits more days than not. For my nineteenth birthday, she and Jude throw me a surprise party at the haus. There are flaming shots. Ursula bakes me cupcakes, tops them in fluffy puffs of cream cheese frosting. I eat one, another. We dance until we're sticky with sweat, giddy. She twirls me, I twirl her, and we could keep twirling like this forever, feet bare on the wood floors, our arms in each other's arms.

Angered by Mateo snagging the cheese position, I go straight to Craigslist: food and bev job listings. I find an ad for a server position in a cheese and wine bar that will be opening soon in Hell's Kitchen. *We work with a constantly changing selection of thirty-five to forty of the best cheeses in the world, each paired with its own housemade accompaniment, to create what we believe will be the best cheese plates in the country.* I send my résumé.

A few days later, I find the spot, on 52nd Street across the street from an outpost of St. Vincent's Hospital that has been slated to close. The narrow storefront smells of dust and acetone. There are drop cloths on the floor and half-painted walls.

"Hi," I say to a man with a power tool. "I'm looking for Brian."

Brian emerges from some kind of trapdoor that leads to a basement. He shakes my hand. "You must be Hannah! As you can see, we're in the middle of building this place."

We sit on crates on the floor, the restaurant a construction project around us, thick with wood smell. A vendor comes in to do a cream and milk tasting, so I join Brian and a woman named Krista in sipping raw milk from little glass jars: silky, sweet, grassy, good.

"I love cheese. I love service. I've never been a server before, only a hostess."

"It's hardly rocket science," Brian says. "The important thing is that you have a brain and you get it. It helps, too, that you love this stuff."

They hire me, and shortly thereafter, Casellula opens. The place is charm filled and narrow, with the kitchen squeezed behind the bar and an antique dresser repurposed as a cheese case. In winter, the windows fog up. Work at The Lula is adrenaline filled and slammed from the start—the sizzle of the panini press, the buzz of service, the no-joke knowledge of the professionals I work beside who are bona fide sommeliers and know their shit deeply, the regulars who come for their midnight goose breast Reuben fix, the parade of ramekins full of blistered Peppadew peppers oozing with buffalo mozz, the late nights, the purple joy of sparkling Shiraz. I am in heaven.

The Lula is the anti-Piche. Rather than a kitchen battalion, there is my friend Jeanie, the chef who works during the day, and a prep cook at night who brings the whole menu to life behind the bar with a panini press, a blowtorch, a lowboy fridge, and a single cutting board.

Everywhere there is cheese. The concept is to unleash the cheese plate from the confines of fine dining, and people love it. Stickers from ninety-pound wheels of Comté and Calvados-washed Camembert cling to the wall. Sheep's milk Wavreumont from Belgium wafts its tangy funk. When the cheese maven Krista takes out a slab of Rogue Creamery Smokey Blue from our cheese case, it's as if someone has lit a campfire. The cheeses are paired with Jeanie's creative, thoughtful condiments: cakes of ancient grains, wild berry jams, spicy dulce de leche.

"What should I wear for service?" I ask Krista, the cheese goddess, before our first night.

"Something cute. Whatever you want." Which is a relief to hear because I still cannot get the muddy cheese smell out of my black Piche blazer, even though it's been to the dry cleaners twice and sprayed with perfume. Everything I wear to my new job will reek of cheese in no time, anyway, but it's nice to work in stretchy jeans, flowy dresses in the summer.

Sunday brunch is the only time that The Lula is ever slow. Jeanie gives me a bowl of cherries to pit up at the bar or fava beans to shell. We play Amy Winehouse and sing along while Jeanie tells me about her estranged mom and the guy she's dating. A few months later, we cancel brunch. The evening service kicks plenty of ass.

I learn my way around this little new restaurant, the way you have to squeeze around the dishwasher when you go to pour some Carmenére at the bar, the way the wines are stacked in boxes in the basement. How to run Manny's food when he is chitchatting with a table he knows from Gramercy.

"Table 7 is industry," Krista says, handing me a plate of gushing triple crème from Four Fat Fowl with beet marshmallows that Jeanie makes in the mornings and stores in the basement with the wine, where it's mucky and cool. Industry people are one of us and get treated as family.

I learn The Lula's rhythms. When we open at five, people start to arrive after work for glasses of sparkling Shiraz and sausages grilled in tortillas and dabbed in milky *crema*. By seven, eight, nine o'clock every table and the blonde wood bar are packed with twosomes on dates. First dates, seconds, anniversaries. I like working behind the bar, where, during the rare times when it's slow, I can eavesdrop and ascertain how the dates are going. It cheers me to see success, shoulders leaning on shoulders, the guttural kind of laughter. But the bad dates are usually the interesting ones.

"Oh my god," I tell Krista as I pick up a plate of blue cheeses, green and gray and nearly purple. She has them plated like a sculpture with wasabi-pickled green beans and taro chips. "B3 says he wants a girlfriend who makes breakfast every morning."

"Good luck to B3," Krista says. "I hope she walks out of here soon."

I cry when Chef Jeanie leaves to cook in Seattle. There is a new interim chef, a beautiful, tall Israeli man named Ari who makes us mushroom flatbreads for family meal. We don't talk much, but he smiles at me knowingly when a difficult customer makes an absurd demand and other times just because.

"Did you see the new hot chef?" my coworker Kati asks me.

"Oh, I saw him," I tell her.

"Well step off, he's mine."

"Ha." She must be joking.

"I'm not joking. I'm claiming him."

Ari leaves me a sliver of chocolate cake above the cheese case, a smiley face in cocoa nibs. "It looks like you need it," he says when I thank him. I've been so exhausted I hurt.

One day I see him slam the basement door in anger.

"Are you okay?"

"I cook because I want to bring people joy. But it's not working here."

"People love the food you cook!"

"It's not my food. It has nothing to do with me."

I have so many questions, but we go back to work.

We never get a chance to really talk. Within weeks, Ari leaves for a job in the kitchen at Per Se, one of the best restaurants in the world. Kati ends up dating the next cook, a gorgeous lesbian with perfect teeth and a radish tattoo.

After the tables of dates go home, together or not together, we get the theater people after their curtains—the cast and crew of whatever is on Broadway and their entourages. Brian briefly dates the musical director of a big show, who comes in nearly every night with gifts for the staff: beaded earrings, Swiss chocolate. After that, at 1 AM, 1:30, the restaurant people arrive. We're near Per Se and the Modern, where Brian and Krista either have worked or just know everybody, and I get to know Lev, who runs the bar program here, and Angela, the GM there, and endless servers and cooks who get what we do and love it.

These final hours prove a challenge. I'm tired in a way I've never been before, an exhaustion that burns my cheeks and hurts my bones. It's finals week the second semester of my sophomore year, and I am working several nights of late shifts at The Lula, from 5 PM until we close at 2 AM. Or rather until we finish cleaning up and filling out paperwork, so more like 3 AM.

It's a Tuesday or maybe a Wednesday and I have been up all night the evening before, writing an epic anthropology paper, and up the night before that, drinking convoluted cocktails with giant-ego'd mixologists who frequent The Lula. I am a person who loves my sleep, and I am running on empty. Or running on caffeine and the toxic fumes of designer gin and steamy pho from the place on the corner, which I scarf behind the cheese station before we open. But none of that adequately substitutes for shut-eye.

The night is one of those perfect spring nights that inspire all New Yorkers at once to get out of their apartments where they have been hibernating all winter and wait however long it takes for a glass of rosé and a wedge of nutty Alpine cheese. The night is relentless. People keep coming and coming and coming. They shove into the door and lean against the windows outside, which are fogged up from panini presses producing grilled cheeses at full capacity. At 1 AM, they are still coming full speed ahead, wanting Grüner Veltliner and brûléed blue cheese and chocolate cake covered with cocoa nibs. It's Manny's own recipe. When we pour fresh cream on top, tableside, some guests let out an actual moan.

Sometime around midnight, I crash.

There are the "on" nights, the seamless nights, when I sail from table to table and pour wine and talk about grilled garlic scapes, when the whole thing is glittery and gratifying and painless. And then there are the "off" nights, or parts of nights, where a semicreepy regular makes my skin crawl with his skeezy suggestions, and I drop a glass or two, and I feel like the last ounce of niceness has been drained from my soul. So I fake it. I take quick breathers and polish silverware and fantasize about making a swift and dramatic exit, but I pull it together and hang in there until it's time to count my cash, down my shift drink, and hail a cab home.

This late, late, maliciously busy night is not like that. I am past grumpy or stressed or groggy. I hit a wall, and big time. It takes every ounce of my willpower just to stand up straight and not collapse on a barstool. I am willing myself to function, but it is not working.

I have a million tables all at once, and I start to forget stuff, which I pretty much never do. I am the queen of dropped plates and shattered glasses (when anyone hears the sound of breaking anywhere in the little restaurant, they sigh "Hannah!" whether or not I am the culprit, which I usually am). But if I say I will bring you some lemon or a glass of pinot blanc, I am good for my word.

But not tonight. I have to take an order for an entire table again, because I forget. Everything. I pop a champagne cork across the room, even though I know to hold the top steady with my thumb, and it hits a tiny woman square between her shoulder blades. She gives me the look of death.

My tables ask for checks, which I fail to deliver. They ask for stinky Meadow Creek Grayson and hazelnut truffles, but their orders are lost on me. My head is swimming and simultaneously empty. I have the spins, as if I'm shitfaced. My back throbs. I am on the brink of tears.

And then, lo and behold, my tables have their cheese, their wine, even their checks. It is an actual miracle. I am falling deep into the shits, and someone has my back.

It is Jamie. Jamie is a superexperienced server, a former dancer with a pixie cut who tells the strangest, dirtiest jokes and brings in her mom's pumpkin seed brittle in a big tin to share with The Lula staff. She sees I am struggling and miraculously comes to my rescue. She has her own tables, her own long list of things to keep up with, but somehow she's managed to also salvage my mess.

"Jamie, thank you!"

"No problem," she says. "You look terrible."

Jamie is my angel. She only comes to my shoulders. She bounces in her sneakers. "Go home," she tells me. I still have all my receipts left to tally, chairs to stack, tables to wipe down. "I got this."

I splurge for a cab and barely make it up the stairs in the haus to my room. I smell like mac and cheese and my hip yelps in mysterious pain. I have a psychoanalytical interpretations of literature exam in six hours.

Morels

I'm back living with my parents for the summer when I wait on a chef at The Lula one late night, during the restaurant-people rush when normal people have been in bed for hours. He comes back the next evening, for Porkslap beer in a pink can and a plate of Krista's favorite cheeses. He is handsome and knows Krista and Manny and everyone else, which happens every night at The Lula. I'm serving him so I get the formal introduction: "This is Connor, he's the Executive Chef at a big deal TriBeCa Restaurant, give him all the love. Connor, this is Hannah. She's all right, too."

Chef Connor asks questions about the cheese and orders another Porkslap. I bring him some speck-wrapped Peppadew peppers on the house. Some goat cheese–hazelnut chocolate truffles, also on the house. He tells me about a new place in the Lower East Side where his friend is cheffing. They serve killer quail, roasted in hay from the same farm.

"Want to go with me tomorrow?"

"Oh, I have to work."

"When do you have a night off?"

"Monday."

"Monday is even better."

Monday night is a bust. The Lower East Side restaurant is dark and sexy, lit up by the flicker of a million candles. Chef Connor's chef friend pulls up a chair and the two men talk for most of our meal of quail roasted in a little hut of hay, morels, fig tart. I may as well not be there. I focus on the morels, which taste as deep as the earth. I'm half-annoyed at being so completely ignored, half-enamored by the smoky morels. When it's time to go, I'm relieved.

"Thanks for dinner, Connor," I tell his baseball hat, pulled over his eyes. "Those morels!"

"I'll drive you home," he offers.

"Oh, it's okay."

"Where do you live?"

"Hoboken."

"I live in Jersey, too. Let me take you."

I refuse again, he insists, holds the door open to his car, which is parked just across the street from the restaurant. I get in. I wish I hadn't. I wish it now, and I wished it then, too. Something feels dangerous inside, maybe the way he doesn't talk to me but grabs my thigh and squeezes it hard.

"Thanks for the ride."

He doesn't say *you're welcome* or *no problem*. He doesn't make small talk.

When we emerge from the dark of the Holland Tunnel on the Jersey side, I tell him, "Turn here." I try to always take the PATH, but I've been tired and splurging for cabs lately, so I know the route to my parents' place even half-asleep.

I am not half-asleep now. His silence unnerves me. He doesn't turn on the radio. He keeps taking one hand off the wheel and gripping my leg, my waist. Should I tell him to stop? I tell myself, *Just get home and then you never have to see him again.* I tell myself, *If he comes to The Lula, Jamie will take his table.*

Connor bypasses the right onto Marin Boulevard that would take us to Hoboken, continues down 78, speeding up into the New Jersey night. The windows are open and the highway's tire-scented air fills my lungs.

"I think you can take the next right and turn around," I suggest. He doesn't make that turn either, only speeds up straight ahead. My discomfort becomes white fear. "Connor, where are we going?"

"Oh, I need to get something at home. Then I'll take you to Hoboken." I try to gauge what he is thinking, but his baseball cap obscures much of his face, which focuses straight ahead.

"Where do you live?" I am hoping for him to say something reassuring, but he doesn't answer.

We drive in silence for what feels like a long time. I want to text someone but I'm not sure what to say. *I'm in a car in who-knows-where New Jersey with a chef, and I'm scared.* He pulls up into a nondescript suburban housing development, kills the ignition. My thighs stick to his leather seats. My heartbeat fills my ears. He rapes me in the parking lot of his home or wherever we are, then drives me to Hoboken. We do not exchange any words.

I am unbearably happy to be home, my parents asleep in their bedroom, my poster of the cheeses of Spain on my wall. I should have taken the PATH. God, how I should have taken the PATH. In the bathroom, I turn the water to scalding and take a long shower, trying to cry quietly so as not to wake up my mom and dad.

When I see Connor seated at The Lula's bar a few weeks later, not late but at 8 PM with a pretty brunette who holds his hand and sips gamay, I have to go outside for a moment and gulp in the 52nd Street air. The restaurant is tiny, and I have to scoot by them every time I talk to table 4. I think he winks at me on his way out, but I'm not entirely sure, even though tonight the baseball cap is turned backward. The last thing I want to do is look at him.

I don't tell anyone about what happened that night, not even Urs, not even the therapist—a woman paid to listen to my problems. In her office, waxy plant leaves snake out the window toward Central Park. I sink into her scratchy sofa. I try to appear as normal and unfucked up as possible.

I never go to the hospital or develop lanugo, soft, downy hair that some anorexics grow, the body's strategy to protect itself against the heat loss that comes with extreme thinness. I don't have heart damage, which I am grateful for. It could have happened. I am one of the lucky ones.

Anorexia is the most fatal mental illness. Deadly. Before a heart stops, way before hospital visits, furry skin, even when the anorexia is merely an idea of itself, a taste of impending famine, it starts to obliterate things. It kills days, nights, dreams. It dims the lights. All the pretty little girls are shrinking, shrinking, degrading their prettiness, turning it upside down, inside out, spitting on it, devouring it, holding it like a knife to their wrists, to everyone else's wrists.

Life whirs its tornadoes of abuses and injustices and miracles. It's wild, unstoppable, brutal. Control is delicious. An eye in the storm. In this little place, in the chasm of my stomach, I can hold the air still as a slick-skinned mannequin. I can stop time. I can count spoonfuls of yogurt, fill my brain with static, hold on for life and for death.

But I am a shitty anorexic, really.

They say there is an anorexic personality: people-pleasing, timid, perfectionistic, inflexible.

And a contrasting bulimic one: impulsive, dramatic, erratic.

I am neither. Or rather, I am all of the above.

Still, sometimes, I look in the mirror and want to hurl or scream.

I chase the fantasy of not-me, calculate escape, bargain, a few hundred calories, a few hundred days, and maybe the pain will not sting me like a jellyfish anymore. In the fantasy, the cosmic guards unshackle me from the prison of my own skin, their whisper hot in my ear: *You are free.*

You are skinny, and you are free.

The whisper never comes.

In the tightly wound logic system of my eating disorder, everything makes perfect sense. Fight loneliness with hunger, smash anger with deprivation, combat heart-sinking pain with the swoosh of the stupid fucking elliptical. Count calories. Sad song on repeat. A small mountain of carrot sticks. Annihilation.

When I started losing weight, I was a rock star. "You look great," I heard from my classmates, cousins, a professor, Corey. *How did you do it? Can you help me?* Men turned around when I passed on the street and followed me with their eyes.

When I tried on a new black dress for The Piche in the Loehmann's communal dressing room once, two older ladies looked me up and down. "We wish we had bodies like yours," they whispered. "You look drop dead in that dress." After a lifetime of hating my body, of never hearing anything like this, it felt both remarkable and ridiculous. I wanted to shake them. I am still the same person. I am still me.

School health services sends me to a nutritionist. Her office is right above the cafeteria, and I hope nobody sees me ascending the steps. The nutritionist wears a baby-blue cardigan that matches her baby-blue shirt. I hate her right away.

I have become haunted by the scale. No number is okay. Whatever it says brings me to tears. The nutritionist weighs me on the scale backward, and for this I am grateful. She gives me a stack of papers with spaces for breakfast, lunch, and dinner—a food diary. I am so good at being the good student, the obedient hostess. My breakfast is coffee, but I write *oatmeal and walnuts*. My lunch is this weird tofu salad I have discovered at the health food store and am obsessed with because a big container has only one hundred calories. (Or says it has one hundred calories? In my paranoia, I wonder if it's mislabeled. How can it only have one hundred calories?) I write down for lunch: *tuna sandwich*. Close enough, I figure. The whole food diary is a lie.

A few weeks in, a turn away from the scale and step on backward. The nutritionist's face contorts into a sour frown.

"Is everything okay?"

"Oh yeah," she says, unconvincingly. "You've just gained a good deal of weight in a week."

The room goes dark and my heartbeat is on a chase. What happened to the backward scale, the secret weigh-in? I hate her. I hate myself.

"Don't worry." It must be obvious, my panic. "Let's just have a look at your food diary. Did you have a big meal before you came here? How are your bowel movements?"

I never eat before facing down (or facing away from) the scale. My bowel movements are fine. The food diary says *oatmeal, tuna sandwich*. In other words, it has nothing to do with what I have actually had to eat.

I tell my therapist, "I don't think I need to see a nutritionist anymore." I tell her what happened last week on the scale.

"There are other nutritionists, if this one is not a good fit," she says, but I have made up my mind. Because my BMI is no longer dangerously low, nobody can force me to see a nutritionist. I have read the whole health section at Barnes & Noble. I can figure out what to eat.

"How is your food?" my therapist asks me most weeks.

"Good! Fine!" I lie.

My therapist is kind, and I do what she says. We talk about reintroducing foods that scare me. I eat pizza once for lunch, a slice of Koronet's as heavy as a textbook, and finish the whole thing. I even sprinkle the fake parmesan from the can on top, some red pepper flakes. The diagnosis on my therapy bills changes to EDNOS: "eating disorder not otherwise specified."

I cry in her office. I know I am getting fatter. What was the point of all this struggle? I gain a few pounds, and nobody says anything ever again to anyone's mom; nobody worries about me. I wish I can say "and then I am cured." I am quite the opposite. I see Steph and Amanda for Jen's birthday only briefly, and Amanda says, "You look so great. I am so glad you are better."

I am not better. If anything, I am worse. I still go as long as I can go without eating, until everything around me breaks into little dots and begins to lose its substance. And then I binge. The binges become longer, more epic, ferocious. I eat as an act of total self-destruction. I lose my iron will to starve myself. I gain weight. I hate myself more than I ever thought possible.

When I go to my parents' place in Hoboken for the occasional long weekend or school break, my dad still scarfs whole bags of pretzels, sleeves of rice cakes. My mom still skips breakfast, her Weight Watchers pamphlets stacked on the kitchen counter with the mail. How am I supposed to recover when they are the same? I eat my meals elsewhere, alone. When my dad says, "I think you're getting better," I hear, "I think you're getting fat." My mom knows better than to bring it up.

While I was losing weight, I felt every detail in my body as if new. I could see blue veins for the first time in my wrists, snaking upward. I stuck a pillow between my knees to sleep, otherwise they knocked together. Under my collarbone, my breastbone emerged. My body was an anatomy lesson. I stood with my feet together to see if there was space between my thighs and there was. These developments surprised and delighted me.

As I gain weight, I stop looking in mirrors. There is no longer space between my thighs, so I stand with my legs wide, not wanting my own excessive flesh to touch itself. It's as if I don't have a body anymore. I focus on ignoring everything below my head.

When I get my period for the first time in eighteen months, my stomach seizes as if in protest. I never had serious cramps before. Now it feels as if all of my insides are contracting. They are turning against me. I bleed clumps of myself, black clots that turn the toilet water inky.

I go through my whole tampon stash in a few days, which I have moved with me from my dorm room to Hoboken to the haus.

I call my mom from the toilet. "I feel like my body is at war with itself. I've never bled like this before."

"Oh sweetie," she says. "Maybe this is your body making up for all that time without a period."

"How do you know that? It doesn't work like that." I hang up the phone. It's not her I resent as much as my failure. This blood is proof. Every month it comes again, less and less violently. Every month a reminder.

I wonder how my therapist knows about my eating disorder, its new incarnation, this EDNOS, this misery. I don't want her to take away my only comfort: my starving, my bingeing, my bingeing, my starving.

I sit on her leather sofa. Tissue boxes are everywhere; the sun seeps in through lateral blinds that clink with the trill of the ceiling fan.

"How's your food?" she asks again.

"Fine." I hate talking about food with her or anyone. "I went to kickboxing at the gym before this. I left feeling shitty about myself."

"Why?"

"Because I couldn't do all of it. It was really hard."

"Isn't that the idea of the class, to challenge you?"

"Maybe. But if I were fitter and better I wouldn't have any trouble banging out burpees all day."

"Isn't that a harsh way of looking at things?"

Is there any other way? I don't need any tissues. Her face looks pretty in the striped light. I wonder if she goes to kickboxing class. I wonder if she ever feels bad about herself. I'm too embarrassed to ask.

I've heard society described as bulimic. I buy it. All and nothing. Extremes, full tilt, full blast. Excess and deprivation and then more excess to ease the agony of all that deprivation. Holiday feasts and New Year's resolutions. Steak dinners and juice cleanses. Cronuts and colonics. Spendspendspend because that thing is going to save the day, save your soul. Sometimes it does. Sometimes the silk of the new dress on your shoulders means you can breathe.

The only thing better than that empty, floaty, powerful feeling of three hundred calories in twenty-four hours is that first bite of chocolate after, cocoa and sugar straight to the brain, hit me, yes yes yesyesyes. And better than that, maybe, the anticipation. All that fierce, exhausting, exhilarating channeling of all the willpower I can muster, and then letting it go, shattering it, the glee of the *fuck it*, the unyoking of myself from myself, from my ruthless taskmaster who taunts and scolds and reviles me all day, every day, chanting "you fat piece of shit" until I vibrate with the echo of its torment.

For a minute, there is chocolate. Only chocolate. Silence and joy and sweetness. Such sweetness.

The cure for anorexia is bulimia. The cure for a diet is a binge. My stomach burns, hollow with its own acid or aching with obscene excess. If only I could walk the tightrope, but over and over again, I fall on my ass.

I am a failed anorexic.

Maybe for six months, eight, I looked a little emaciated. My freshman year and into my sophomore fall. If you saw me then, you might have wondered. But probably you wouldn't have. Some people are thinner, and others are curvier. People have dainty ankles and others puffy cankles. Bubble butts and no butts. They say be grateful to have a butt at all, legs that run, arms that hug. I am grateful. And still, it's painful, living here. There is no escape.

Maybe if you knew me well, you would see that in any given few months I was a different size, that I gained and lost weight faster than my wardrobe or brain could keep up. (In my closet: size two, size six, size twelve). But maybe you didn't see anything at all. I like wearing layers, stretchy pants. Anyway, we would be talking fast, about Berlin and boys with chef's knife tattoos and Bravo TV. Nobody knew that I bought a dozen protein bars last night (A box! A bodybuilder's breakfasts for a week!), took a single, frantic bite of each one, and threw the rest away, stalling my own massacre the only way I could, fighting my eating disorder with a brain full of deafening disorder.

You can't see an eating disorder. Thin people, fat people, normal people have this thing. We look like you. We laugh like you and run to the subway and belt out karaoke and catch ourselves social media-ing when we should be working. We eat dinner with you like a normal person eats dinner—fork, knife, glass of red, smiles. Maybe at night, at home, we eat another dinner, another four dinners, and maybe we don't. Maybe we throw up and maybe we don't. Maybe we wake up at 5 AM to feel our foot soles against the pavement to run away from those dinners, ourselves. And maybe we don't.

We share the torment, though. Our bodies are different, and our bodies are fine. Underweight, overweight, they are fine. But our brains, our hearts, our spirits are aching, crying out—help me help me help me.

I am empty of everything I crave: good food, meaning, love. My notebooks of poems and stories are long gone. Instead, I have reams of pages of calorie counts, logs of apples and bananas and readings from the scale. I have lost and gained the mass of a small army. But mostly I have lost myself.

During the three years I live in the haus at 114th Street, sophomore, junior, and senior years of college, I spend long, lovely hours in its kitchen. It is my territory, though I share it with my housemates. It is escape, and glorious.

The Vulcan is not just its hearth but its heart. She is the size of a car. Twelve burners grace her top. Her presence is a throwback to when the house was home to a dozen rich, white fraternity boys, and their chef lived in the basement and cooked up breakfast, lunch, and dinner in her powerful oven-belly. The Vulcan is rusty, dirty, cranky, and temperamental. She is beautiful.

The best part of being a member of the Society is living in its house, even in a lofted bed up close and personal to a pipe that screams and wails and clatters all night. The alumni remind us: "Never again will you live in such an incredible place in Manhattan," and we know they are right. They knock on the door to room 32 and say, "I had a lot of sex in that bed. Damn, did I have a lot of sex in that bed," and I laugh and try not to think about it. A taxidermy moose that Teddy Roosevelt purportedly shot hangs above our big fireplace. A sticky bar is outfitted with leather stools, a chalkboard that usually has something obscene scrawled across it. Coming home to a lopsided fire, I know I am lucky. It burns whenever we have wood; the smoke turns the moose's fur stringy and sallow.

Taylor, Dan, Jude, and everyone else sit around the fire, spread out with piles of laptops and books and Two Buck Chuck in giant mugs. I don't have biological brothers and sisters, but I have these guys. "How was your exam?" they ask when I have an exam. I am touched that they remember. Dan cuts out an article about stinky cheese and slips it under my door.

Everyone's friend's brother's band plays in the living room. We have poetry readings and parties that last all weekend and "spiritual gatherings" on the fire escape when the weather turns warm, with chanty music and great plumes of marijuana and towering cakes with many, many layers we bake in the middle of the night.

For some reason, I only see Taylor between the hours of 1 AM and 6 AM. He's from Kansas, and so we make BBQ sauce for fifty pounds of chicken at 2 AM to feed everyone the next day in our tiny backyard from a single, pitiful grill. I follow his instructions; he lets me wear his prized "Kansas" apron for the occasion.

With Iva, who came from New Orleans, I make gumbo and dirty rice. With David, plantains and chicken piccata. Brenna fries falafels in a sputtery mess of oil; I help her brush phyllo with butter for baklava. Jess teaches me how to cook her grandmother's tomato sauce. We watch the tomatoes bubble away for hours atop the Vulcan, chopping onions that make us tear up and mountains of red peppers, drinking cheap wine, and dancing to Lily Allen.

On my restricting days, I eat none of it, downing Diet Coke until I feel like I may drown in tannic carbonation. On my bingeing days, I first eat everything I can without drawing attention to myself, and then stop, scared of who is watching. Dan sniffs too much coke, Taylor has a bong as tall as he is, and Tim almost kills himself coming down from an acid trip, although he says his suicidal imaginings are just flirtations. I tell myself everyone has their thing, their drug—it could be worse—as I eat the last plate of pasta, spoon the last icing into my mouth, look for what else I can devour.

The summer after my junior year, I get an internship at *Serious Eats*. Food blogs are still new and thrilling, and *Serious Eats* is one of a few big guns that people pay attention to. I interview with Ed, the founder, who asks about my bagel preferences—chewy or fluffy—what my last meal would be. I guess I answer to his satisfaction. I get the internship.

On my first day, the web guy sits with me and walks me through the basics of putting up a post on WordPress, some starter HTML. The office is usually shrouded in a thick field of quiet, everyone typing at their desks with headphones on, the opposite of restaurantland. We communicate via chat on our screens even though we sit next to each other. The quiet morphs into happy tumult for shipments of blue cheese ice cream and soft pretzels, everyone huddling around to partake and discuss. Twice a week, we gather to blind taste test something for an article: chunky peanut butter and vanilla cake mix (prepared), hot sauce, granola. I scoop out the food of the day onto white paper plates, label them with numbers, arrange them on our conference table. We grade on taste and texture. Before and after, Ed leads us in long investigations into the Platonic ideal of a chocolate chip cookie, say, a sparerib, a vanilla milkshake. "How can you say this is the perfect chocolate chip cookie if we don't know the specifics of that perfection? Chewy or crispy? Moist or crumbly? Chips or chunks? What is the right cookie-to-chocolate ratio?"

Our seriousness about food comes first from love. We dream about soup dumplings. Superb tacos will make the difference between a good day and a shitty one. We have positioned our lives to let us be here, debate chocolate chip cookie density for a living. And second, because our readers trust us. They will buy new peanut butter based on our word, make something fantastic or disappointing for dinner depending on our recipe, and we can't bear the thought of ruining someone's dinner, even a side dish, even a jar of peanut butter, a vanilla milkshake.

We go on field trips, too. At a new Italian spot in Williamsburg after work on a Tuesday, Ed and a few of us order every single dish on the menu, tasting, passing, pausing for Robyn to snap showstopping photos, discussing. We take the 7 train to Queens for papaya salad with blue crab at SriPraPhai Thai and spicy Korean wings at Unidentified Flying Chickens. As an intern, I head to the original Shake Shack whenever they change a custard flavor to wait and wait on line and bring back everyone in the office Shack burgers and custards. Ed hates the fries and writes Danny Meyer an open letter, proclaiming this. A few weeks later, the Shake Shack fries get a makeover.

The freezer is so full of ice cream it must be hip checked to close. The cabinets are full of cereal and Japanese candies and artisanal corn chips, and the conference table is so covered in croissants and pastrami sandwiches and Armenian string cheese we cannot see any actual table.

I eat all these things. The communal nature somehow assuages my eating-disordered brain. Everyone in the office is in it together, holding translucent pieces of bresaola up to the light that comes from 7th Avenue, chewing slowly. I am just doing my job. Anyway, it is just a bite, then another bite. At the end of the day, I'm grateful that I have no idea how many bites I took of what.

At night, though, after work, a cool breeze of fear often wafts its way around me. My jeans don't zip. It's summer, so I wear silky dresses and skirts that stretch and move with me and my expanding tummy. Between our marathons of gnocchi and Szechuan noodles and street cart lamb and rice I eat less and less raw veggies from the salad bar near the office, fruit salad from the bodega. Even this I feel guilty about.

When Josh and I meet, he still goes by Mr. Cutlets. He is writing for *Grub Street*, the *New York* magazine food blog he founded. *Grub Street*, *Serious Eats*, and *Eater* are *the* food blog rivals of 2008. The competition is friendly, we say, and to prove that, we all get together at the Red Hook Ball Fields to feast on *pupusas* and *arepas*. It is high summer and unkindly hot. We order one of everything, spread out on the green grass, and eat our faces off. After, Robyn and an *Eater* photo editor come back with boxes of key lime pies dipped in chocolate from Steve's.

We are full of slow-cooked goat meat and the sunshiny sugar of key lime when the skies unleash a wild downpour. Josh knows where to go: dark, divey Sunny's, where we drink cold beer, laugh, digest, and dry. Nobody has an umbrella. My sandals stick to my feet, my dress to my thighs.

"Can we go out for a drink?" Josh asks me. "And are you twenty-one?"

"I'll be twenty-one in no time."

Josh has just turned forty-one. He takes me to the late, great Alto for my twenty-first birthday, where we eat hunks of lardo and ribbons of veal ragù–laced pasta. I wear the black dress I sometimes wore to work at The Piche. The back is so low I had to cover myself with a jacket in the dining room during service—I had to wear a jacket anyway—but tonight I am jacketless. He brings me his latest book, *The Hamburger: A History.* In the front cover he has inscribed, *Dear Hannahleh, don't stop writing. You're good. Happy birthday.*

After dinner, the chef Michael White pulls up a chair at our table, and we all drink sambuca and laugh until the table next to us gives us dirty looks.

We make it to PDT by midnight, the "secret" bar on St. Marks. Josh knows these guys, too, of course, and we beeline past the waiting crowds to the singular corner table, drink champagne. He puts his hand somewhere midback where my dress ends, and I feel my heartbeat under his meaty palm. I'm twenty-one and the luckiest girl in the world. He kisses me and kisses me until he hails a cab for me home to 114th Street. I am twenty-one and an official grown-up. Out the window, the city flashes and glitters like candles on the most magnificent cake.

The next day he texts, *You're much too young for me, Hannahleh.* Josh calls me *Hannahleh,* like he is some old Yiddish man, which he sort of is. *Let's go for a meatball.*

Instead, we go to a glitzy restaurant at a snazzy hotel on the East Side. He says he needs to write about it. Before meeting him there, I stand in my closet for forever, worried about what to wear. Nothing is right. Urs comes over with a greenish dress, and it just barely fits. She zips me up.

Black boots, eyeliner. Dan says I look sexy, but he is so high his eyes are liquid.

At the restaurant, the walls are golden and a grand staircase ascends and ascends. The manager comes to shake Josh's hand, the bartender comes from behind the bar to shake his hand, the chef comes out from the kitchen to shake his hand. He kisses me on the cheek, then on the mouth. We order truffled things and foie gras, and I think I can die now.

"Are you still hungry?" Josh says on Park Avenue afterward. A siren wails, and I have to shout my response.

"A little." I'm always hungry these days.

"I know just the thing." First, we smoke from his one-hitter. The siren passes, and the city smells like metal, exhaust, heat.

Josh can't believe that I have never been to Steak 'n Shake. "I'll order for us," he says. He gets us three double 'n cheese burgers, a vanilla shake, and a strawberry shake. It is late and Steak 'n Shake is nearly empty. We take our bounty to the back. Josh feeds me burger, his hands up to my mouth, and it is both glorious and repugnant. "You're hot," he tells me. Meat juice dribbles down my chin. He kisses me. I can't stop laughing. I nearly spit up my milkshake.

Josh is a big guy. He's overweight by any sort of measure. I like the way I am small by comparison standing next to him. I like the way he shakes when he laughs, laughs with his whole body, the way his eyes squint and water.

He writes about having gout, "I won't be altering my lifestyle at all, and that you can continue to expect the up-to-the-minute coverage of the city's dining scene that only total bodily dedication can bring." I respect this commitment. The food world expresses its horror and delight in a flurry of blog posts. I am glad nobody is blogging about my body. I am less skinny than I used to be.

Josh is everything I want to be: welcome in all of New York's best restaurants, a bon vivant, a brilliant, famous writer. And he is everything I fear: fat.

"Come to Ozerkastan," Josh asks, and I say yes. Ozerkastan is Ditmas Park, way out in Brooklyn where he claims he has been exiled. He picks me up from the haus in his rattling car. On the way to Ozerkastan, we stop at Fairway in Red Hook for steak and olive oil. I drive the shopping cart. We both like Gata-Hurdes, green as grass in its bottle.

"You have nice arms, Hannahleh," he tells me back in the car. "Everyone must say that."

I've never heard anyone say I have nice arms. I look at my arms. Maybe they are not so terrible. I roll down the window.

His apartment is cozy, and the walls are covered in paintings he tells me are the work of his dead father. They are full of sweeping lines and feeling. "Your father was incredibly talented." I'm standing in front of a painting of a chef in Josh's dining nook. The chef's face and toque are but wisps. The chef stirs a dark, deep pot that is the focus of the painting, full of something red and thick and bubbling.

"My dad was a stagehand at a casino in Atlantic City. He was seething with spirit, and his art was his only way to channel anything. Which makes it all the more sad that he was a complete failure." I love Josh's stories. He doesn't seem to hold back.

Josh makes us the lemon pasta Michael White taught him to cook. "Mikey said it was the simplest pasta ever, which is something only a chef would say. Something only the Sultan of Spaghetti would say." I find it endearing, how completely Josh focuses on salting his water and zesting his lemon. The pasta is good, but he is sure Michael White would have made it many times better. We pour the Gata-Hurdes all over the pot like sauce. I note that Josh is a famous glutton, and I can keep up with him bite for bite, no problem. I am jealous of Josh. I want to be a famous glutton.

Josh calls Éric Ripert "the Ripper" and Anne Burrell "Man Burrell." Scott Conant is just "Scotty." We eat at all their restaurants. It's not like eating at a restaurant as a normal person—there is an endless procession of dishes, refilled glasses, handshakes, hugs, nuggets of chef gossip. I am both thrilled to be a part of this world and aware that I am not a part of this world at all. I am peripheral. I am a visitor. This is a giant club, a fraternity, and I am not a member. I get a smile if I'm lucky. Nobody asks how I am or what I'm up to. It's Josh they care about.

I resent this entirely, but my resentment gives me a sort of energy. I write and write for *Serious Eats* and whoever else will publish me. One day I will be in the center of this world. They won't tell me, side-eyed, "Oh, you're Josh's friend." They will say to Josh, "You must be Hannah's friend." And he will nod and say, "I knew her way back when."

I care about Josh, too. He's scary smart and talks how he writes, throwing around big words and obscure references to 1960s intellectuals. "I wanted to be a public intellectual, but I was doomed to languish in obscurity. Better to be a B-list food person than a C-list intellectual," Josh says over pasta. Josh tells me how, on his way to Mr. Cutlets, he lived in upstate New York and wrote copy for an automotive trade publication. He was married and divorced. He has an unfinished doctorate in American History and wrote a book about Archie Bunker and that book about hamburgers.

Josh is grandiose and sometimes tormented. He calls bacon a "straight-up fetish object." He is a purist glutton—there can never be enough meat, drugs, booze, excess, celebrities, and big, obscure words. We wait on line like everyone else for Di Fara pizza, watch Dom DeMarco snip off basil from a giant bouquet and anoint his pies with olive oil that he pours from what looks like a genie bottle. We eat our pizza for breakfast the next morning, with leftover steak from Minetta Tavern that Josh fries in butter. We go to parties with Anthony Bourdain and the meat god Pat LaFrieda Jr. and Geoffrey Zakarian. There is a group of superskinny ladies in small dresses at these parties, their hair ironed straight.

"Who are they?" I ask Josh.

"Oh, those are the chef groupies." How can the chef groupies be so impossibly thin? Is that part of the appeal? Why wouldn't they choose rock stars like normal groupies? Josh squeezes my hand.

"I'm so exhausted," Josh complains after a three-hour feast on the secret/not secret third floor of the Spotted Pig. "I love this, don't get me wrong. But sometimes I just want to be a normal person."

Josh loves being recognized, being important. He loves it more than anything. "You don't want to be a normal person."

"You're totally right. But one day a week to watch TV with you in Ozerkastan and eat spaghetti isn't enough."

"Well, what are you doing Tuesday?"

It turns out Tuesday is a Halloween party in the sprawling Daniel kitchen. Daniel Boulud gives me a big hug, as if we go way back. There is a whole suckling pig laid out on a table, more food than seems possible, a bowl of punch the size of a bathtub. The pastry chef is putting the finishing touches on a cake taller than me. Every famous food person is here dressed as French toast, as a bunny, as Dr. Seuss. Josh didn't mention this was a costume party; we are costumeless.

I am jealous of Josh's career, of the way he knows everyone. I want to be invited to secret parties by big-deal chefs. I want to write things people talk about.

I try to mingle. People are drunk and friendly and soon, so am I. The pig is soft and rich as pig butter. It's 3 AM when we decide to cab to Ozerkastan. Ditmas Park is not so close. I fall asleep on Josh's shoulder.

"Shit," he says, finally outside his apartment door. "Shit."

"What?" I am drunk and sleepy.

"I don't have my keys."

"Oh shit. It happens to the best of us."

We consider a locksmith but decide instead to cab back to the haus. I've moved out of my bunk bed in 32 with Jude and have my very own room, so I decide it'll be fine.

"This place is wild," he says, stumbling up the spiral staircase. Taylor and a guy I don't know are drinking beers at the second-floor bar, and they wave. My new room is tiny and we barely fit inside. It is cold outside but the heat chugs on in the haus. The old pipes creak. I open my window as far as it will go. Still, we are both sweaty. I fit myself around the mass of him on my creaky twin bed. His skin smells like pig and whiskey. We pass out.

Josh is gone when I wake up.

"Who is the old guy who left your room this morning?" Dan asks.

"That's Josh. *The* Josh. Mr. Cutlets."

"Oh my god, he's old," Dan says. I punch Dan on the shoulder. "Just telling it how it is." I know he's right.

Josh calls that afternoon. "Hannahleh, I'm sorry I snuck out. How are you feeling?"

"I've felt better." My head feels as if someone's filled it with seltzer and shook it up. I am hungover and full of regret about the buttery biscuits I ate last night, the fluffy cake, the damn pig.

"Hannahleh, being in that house made it glaringly clear. I have no business being in that house. I have no business dating you. I'm way too old for you."

He's said it before, but I know it is different this time. I know a breakup call when I hear it. "We will always be friends. Always." Maybe it's just a line, but I feel it to be true.

I'm weepy and hungover that night. I knock on Dan's door, but there is no answer. I text him, *I'm sad. So sad.*

Where are you? he responds in seconds.

Home.

Give me 15. Don't move.

Dan jumps into my bed and wraps me in a hug. He has brought *Vogue, New York* magazine, *Vanity Fair*, his glass bowl. "We're going to read magazines and smoke until you feel better. Then we're going to get some sleep."

"Fine. I don't want *New York* magazine, though. Josh has a story in this issue."

Dan throws the magazine off the bed and into my trash can.

"Better," I say. "Also, thank you for this. I love you."

"I love you, too. Maybe you should date someone closer to your age . . ."

"Ugh. Do you have any snacks?"

Dan keeps a blue plastic bin of vanilla wafers and tortilla chips under his desk. We polish everything off in my bed, leaving crumbs on my sheets and in my hair.

We're throwing our last New Year's party in the haus to ring in 2009, the year we will graduate.

"You're so marriageable," Dan tells me.

"Ha!" I say. "Tell that to the cooks." Dan knows about everything with Josh and Damien and the Executive Chef. I am braising short ribs, and we have run out of pots. We are expecting thirty or so guests tonight, including Dan's boyfriend Jake, who is flying in from Oxford.

"You could do this, like, professionally. Marry some fabulously wealthy, disgustingly brilliant magnate and cook incredible feasts for a rotating cast of intellectuals and artists and such."

"I never considered that career path."

"Well consider it, sister. That smells incredible."

Dan is uninterested in helping me cook but awesome at providing Diet Cokes and lightning-fast conversations. We already have answers before the questions.

I am getting sentimental—the last New Year's on 114th Street—until a gigantic cockroach shimmies from a drawer. Dan laughs at me when I shriek, but then I scoop it into a paper towel, flush it down the toilet.

I can't find a ladle. Where did our pots go?

I'll have to braise in lots of batches. The Vulcan's insides are full of short ribs, bubbling, perfuming the air with dense, meaty goodness.

Rib Eye

Joining the steakhouse is like joining the military. The propaganda is heavy-handed. "This is the best restaurant in the world," they say with a straight face, but I find that hard to believe. I've graduated with my degree in anthropology and don't know what else to do. They have a management training program and a corporate ladder. It feels like a way to turn my restaurant love into a grown-up, respectable career.

The steakhouse serves ribs in a mess of sweet, gloppy sauce and grinds their own beef for hamburgers every day. It's absolutely respectable. They have an incredible operation. But best restaurant? Hardly. I've eaten Daniel Boulud's suckling pig in his own basement. I've had the eleven-course tasting at Eleven Madison Park.

Like the military, the steakhouse moves their recruits around. "Every six to eighteen months for the first five years of employment." They have spots in New York and Chicago, Boston and San Francisco. During my interview, this sounds like an adventure.

They call to tell me I'm going to Pasadena for boot camp—this four-month training.

"TJ, the GM there, is a superstar. And they have an amazing koi pond in Pasadena."

Before I leave New York for Pasadena, I need to buy my new work wardrobe, mandated black suit, white shirt, kitchen clogs, hair pulled back—"No flyaways! Use more hair spray!"—no jewelry, no nail polish—it might chip into a fifty-dollar rib eye. (As a manager, I get armed with a bottle of hair spray. I am to dole out spritzes to employees with out-of-place hair.)

I try on a fitted blazer in a size my brain tells me is respectable—a four or a six at Banana Republic—and nope! Not at all. The fabric doesn't come close to encircling my torso, my stupid boobs, my too-broad shoulders. I put the jacket back on the hanger and flee as fast as I can.

I'm empty-handed but stuck with the knowledge that I've gained some scary, unspecified amount of weight since my anorexic phase. (The scale would be unthinkable. Even walking by the one in the gym locker room makes my palms sweat.) I no longer fit into my aspirational sizes. At home, I sink onto my floor, my butt on hard floorboards. This time, it's cushiony as a sofa. I think of how much better I feel physically, how much more forgiving this softer body is. Yet I'm struck catatonic by my defeat. It's made no difference, the leaves of lettuce, the beige, bunless veggie patties, the growling emptiness in my stomach, everywhere. I thought I could pay for skinniness in the currency of self-hatred. I'm filthy rich with it. And here I am, back where I started all those years ago.

"I don't know what to do," I tell my therapist, feeling like I may drown in my own failure. My dream is still of thinness, and, having reached it once, I have so quickly undone all of my grueling work. I longed to start my life in New York skinny, and I did. I want to start my Los Angeles life skinny just as badly, and it's slipping away fast. I'm leaving in a month. I'm leaving in a week. That Banana Republic jacket that cinches in and in at the waist is no closer to fitting. (I've visited again. Even the eight was uncomfortably tight.)

The therapist gives me what turns out to be solid advice for now and always: "Screw the size. You need clothes for your new job. Sizes are arbitrary, anyway. It doesn't matter if you are a zero or a sixteen. It matters that you have something to wear that fits and that you feel good in. Try to leave your ego aside and just go get some black suits."

Dan and I cry a bit, packing up the haus. Dan is going straight to grad school at Harvard to study medieval literature. It seems as good a plan as any. We stay up all night before graduation, smoking and reminiscing.

"Do you remember when I had to wake you up from the fire escape?"

"Of course! What about the time we were so high in Eastern lit we giggled all class?"

"But you saved us by arguing that passage in *The Upanishads* was hilarious."

"And when Taylor climbed out the window onto the flagpole and couldn't get back?"

"I remember everything."

In the morning, I can't find my tassel anywhere. Everyone's parents traipse through the haus after graduation. We serve tiny catered sandwiches.

My parents wrap me up in a happy hug. My favorite professor says, "Don't stop writing," his forehead glistening in the May heat. I am taken aback by how much this means to me. My GPA is a big, respectable number. Yet I know I have failed utterly. My thighs rub together under my sky-blue gown, and I avoid everyone's family's cameras. When my own ask for a picture, I concede to just one with Dan. When the day is over, I am relieved.

I fly to LA with my biggest suitcase full of black suits in sizes that I will myself to ignore.

Urs flies out a week later. I drive to the airport in my new car, a blue Beetle I bought used, online, and picked up from the dealership after landing in my new hometown. The cantaloupe-colored plastic flower on the dash makes me smile. Until this week, I had never even visited LA. I had envisioned a sea of sunshine and blond hair, but there are all kinds of people, and when I arrive, the sky is gray, as if someone sucked all the color out. In the distance, plumes of smoke crest the sky. The forest fires, this season, are insane. The air is so dry that my wavy hair falls stick straight to my shoulders.

I am an unconfident driver, and the 110 is clogged with chaos of big trucks and big traffic. When I finally arrive at LAX, I am flush with nerves and nausea.

With Urs in the passenger seat, the ride home is infinitely better. The city looks more graceful. We head to Ikea and eat gravlax, buy some colorful plates for my kitchen, mirrors to hang on the wall, a table, a lamp. At a thrift store we find two oversized office chairs with plush leather seats. They're perfect and cheap, but we can't quite fit them into my Beetle. Two guys help us in the parking lot, and we just manage to close the trunk. Urs has to pull her seat all the way up and rides with her legs squeezed under her, the chair rattling like a maraca as we drive back to Pasadena.

This is my first home and everything is perfect because everything is mine. There's a tiny porch where I drink my coffee in the morning and stand watch over the endless traffic. There's a communal pool and a hot tub bordered by a rickety fence and palm trees where I go once with Ursula and then never again because I can't stand the idea of putting on a bathing suit. I've kept my blue bikini from Portugal, and on brave days I try it on, until the back strap snaps and its little beads fall to the floor with melodic clinks.

I've never lived near palm trees, and they make me feel like I'm on perpetual vacation, even when I'm shaky from loneliness.

But for now, Ursula is here. Urs has a friend in LA. One of my brothers from the haus grew up here, and another one is passing through on a layover. That's officially enough guests for a housewarming, I decide.

In preparation, we fill up the cart at Whole Foods: fish, crema, avocado for fish tacos, bottles of bubbly and rosé because they sell wine in grocery stores in California, ingredients for Urs's famous butter-crusted lemon bars for dessert, bags of crystalized ginger and yogurt-covered almonds and tortilla chips for snacking. I spend the rest of my signing bonus—what I haven't used on chairs and rent—on goodies. We get lost in the parking lot trying to leave, looping in endless loops until Urs saves the day and gets us out of there.

Everyone comes over that night, taking over the leather office chairs and the floor. Someone brings a big bag of weed, because this is California. We cook and drink until our heads are light as balloons. We open the doors to the porch and the wind serenades us. My friends, my life, my home. Palm trees out the windows. Laughter like redemption. I think being grown-up might be okay.

A few days later, Urs says goodbye and I start work. It is a busy restaurant—a ruthlessly busy, successful restaurant—though I never quite understand the universality of its appeal. Is it the ribs, which Morning Prep Cook #2 dips one by one in a vat of bacon fat? The promise of absolute by-the-book consistency? The designer fishies swimming in the pond by the entrance? Sure, the steaks are fine and the lighting impeccably lovely, but there are so many more places to dine in New York and LA, Chicago and DC, places with more soul and less hair spray.

Still, there are business lunches and business dinners. A famous rapper, always with a posse and a bodyguard who sits at the bar and drinks pineapple juice. Families with kids who fling French fries all over the floor. First dates with men who look serious and women with their hair ironed slick.

"How did you like living in LA?" friends will inquire, later, but the truth is, I could have been anywhere. I barely notice the nectar sun on my face, the San Gabriel Mountains cresting behind me. I work a minimum of sixty-hour weeks, and my shifts are at odd times. I close the restaurant, stumble home drunk on exhaustion at 2 AM, and get up at 5 AM to open the restaurant the next day. "It builds character," they tell the three management trainees. I am grateful for Andras and Liz, who seem almost as miserable as I am. Liz moved here from New Haven and Andras loves to drive his dad's Porsche into the LA sunshine. Andras has a way with sucking up to TJ. The single time we have a day off together, we head to Liz's apartment, gossip, drink rosé. We wouldn't be friends otherwise, but the steakhouse makes for strange partnerships.

We are each scheduled to work for twelve hours, but if we leave after twelve hours, it is seen as some kind of moral failing. "Where are you going?" the GM barks. "Do you think these knives are going to sharpen themselves?" When he's angry, he makes us polish the copper detailing beside the open kitchen. He's angry a lot.

Right away, I have tests. Newly liberated from school, I am now memorizing the thirty-six varieties of single malts behind the bar, the biography of the artist who sculpted the giant sculpture behind the koi pond, and the temperature of medium-rare (130 to 135 degrees Fahrenheit). There are three binders full of rules and then they give me more binders full of recipes and best practices and service standards, and I worry that the binders are never-ending. At home, they fill half of my new bookshelf.

Training managers learn the ropes by working for a week or two in every restaurant position. At the "service bar"—there is a bar where guests congregate, and a whole other bar that makes drinks for the dining room—the senior management tests me by ordering up margaritas, Rob Roys, and Sazeracs. I have a crush on Yashar the service bartender, an Iranian comedian, but managers are strictly prohibited from "fraternizing with employees."

He shows me his glass polishing method—warm the rag with steam from the cappuccino machine. Use elbow grease. "Put the polished glasses here and the dirty glasses there. Polished glasses go to the nice guests, dirty to the nasty ones."

"Are you serious?"

Like all the service bartenders, he is dressed entirely in black. The lights dimming for dinner service give the effect of his body receding into the restaurant as if he is just a face and a rag. The cappuccino machine lets out a puff. "You can tell the nasty guests because they have children or bodyguards or both," he whispers conspiratorially, leaning in, straight-faced.

I giggle.

"Good," he says. "This place may steal our life, but we can't let it steal our laughter."

It is refreshing to laugh in this restaurant that takes itself so seriously. We smile as we polish, holding the glasses up to check for smudges.

I'm used to living with twenty people, more with everyone's friends and boyfriends and little sisters around. My apartment is quiet, even when I flip on the TV. The quiet startles me.

I am about to turn twenty-two and realize I don't know anyone to invite to celebrate with me. My birthday is a rare day off work, and I try to distract myself. I drive to Santa Monica and go for a walk along the boardwalk, the ocean nearly still below me, the Ferris wheel above. I buy myself beets and cara cara oranges and pink flowers at the farmers market. I don't have a vase, but they look festive in a mug on my kitchen counter. My mom calls, my dad calls, but I reverberate with sadness.

When I get home, there is a box from Urs at my doorstep. I nearly cry out with joy. I rip it open. There are dangly earrings which I hang on my ears, two fancy chocolate bars that I eat right there, over the packaging and her postcard, its loopy scrawl declaring her love.

I find the fat bags of crystalized ginger and yogurt-covered almonds that Urs and I bought still in my cabinet and have just one bite, just another bite, until the sweets are gone and my tongue is dry and achy.

I think about curling up and going to sleep, but I put on a white sundress and take myself to a bar within walking distance because I only turn twenty-two once and driving still stresses me out, especially at night, especially half-drunk on chocolate and sugar. There are muscly guys in tank tops sidled up to the bar. They look like they have just come from the gym. I order a glass of prosecco. I start talking to one of them.

The bartender asks for my ID and hands it back. "This one's on the house. Happy birthday!"

"It's your birthday?" Tank Top Number One asks.

He buys me a shot. Then they all buy me a shot. I'm happy that someone is celebrating my birthday.

I'm not used to such a quick deluge of tequila, and I have to run outside to throw up into the little plot of grass in the parking lot. My body lets out a torrent of half-digested tequila and salt and crystalized ginger and candy-coated nuts. The release feels both awful and satisfying. It is just getting dark, and an older couple, holding hands, stares at me with unfettered disgust.

I feel a hand on my shoulder. Tank Top has come outside to check on me. I am touched by the gesture.

"I'm sorry," he says. "It was a lot of tequila. Are you okay?"

"Never been better." I wipe my lips with the back of my hand, embarrassed.

"Want a ride home?"

"No, thank you. I can walk."

Never again will I let a man I don't know and don't trust drive me home.

"No way," he says. "It's your birthday! I would never pull anything sketchy. You need a ride, trust me."

I realize I can't walk particularly well. Everything is swirly and fluid, as if in a hologram. A ride from a stranger feels safer than making my way home without one, I guess.

He has a big truck full of coffee cups and piles of papers, which he moves carefully out of the way of the passenger seat. He buckles my seatbelt for me and knows where to turn off of Arroyo Boulevard when I tell him the name of my apartment complex. I think I may have to throw up again and open the window, but I hold it together until he pulls up in front of my place, opens the door for me.

"Happy birthday!"

"Thank you for taking me home," I tell him before I barf my guts out on the spindly trunk of a palm tree. I manage to set my alarm for 5 AM before passing out. Tomorrow I work the opening shift.

In the fluorescent glare of my bathroom, I put on my stupid black suit and black clogs. When I walk, they stick and unstick to my heel with every step. I think about all of those calories in the candy I inhaled, am relieved I left it all in a vile mess in the parking lot beside the palm tree. I finger the space between my pants and my skin, the small gap in the waistband. Am I losing weight? I allow myself to feel giddy with the possibility. I am starting to hate this place, but maybe twenty-two will be not just the year I become skinny, but the year I manage to stay that way.

Dishwashing isn't so bad, the swoosh of the machine almost meditative. The percussive clack of stacking plates, the clear cling of silverware. My hands get used to the steaming hot plates. My brain enters a sort of dishwashing chant—*rinse, load, unload.*

I like doing the prep in the morning—mixing big bowls of barbecue sauce and brownie batter and singing show tunes with the bodybuilding prep cook, his muscles bulging through his starched chef whites. We sing *Fiddler on the Roof* songs while we chop and stir.

"You should wear gloves," he advises while I slice mountains of garlic into slivers.

"Why?"

"Your boyfriend won't love it when you reek of garlic."

"I don't have a boyfriend."

"Well you won't get one, smelling all garlicky."

I learn how to pop out the pit of an avocado with the heel of my knife, score its flesh with the skin on, then peel away to reveal perfect wedges. I braise cabbage, deglazing with a plume of vinegar that makes the kitchen thick with cabbage smoke.

The senior meat cooks are meat geniuses. A dozen rib eyes, strips and filets, more, licked by an open flame. (When I open the restaurant, I stoke the wood that will fuel the day and night's steaks.) Each steak must be a perfect example of medium-rare, medium-well, black 'n blue.

"How do you know that's rare?" I ask the night's meat cook, who flips a filet mignon onto a white plate, its canvas, without a second look.

I've read about the feel of the thing, that a medium-rare steak should give like the soft spot between your thumb and fingers when you make a soft fist.

"I can see it," he says.

"Really?"

"I can hear it, too. You have to listen to the meat. Watch it. It's talking."

"Wow."

"Also, I've been cooking steak for fifteen years."

At first, I love the profundity of my exhaustion when I come home, the satisfaction of the ache in the arches of my feet, my lower back, proof I have worked. I sink into my bed as if into the abyss. I never want to get up.

One night after work, I am half-asleep when I get a Facebook request from Ari. It takes me a beat to remember who he is . . . Ari, the movie-star gorgeous cook from The Lula. I remember his seriousness and how his family meals were the best family meals. Why is he messaging me? It's been several years, and at The Lula we rarely talked. Why not? I am lonely in Pasadena. I type my hello. We start chatting. I type, wait a beat, type.

Are you Jewish? he asks me over Facebook message, with a smiley emoji.

Yup, I write.

Good, he says. *We can get married. Lol.* This time his smiley winks at me on my computer screen, asymmetrical. I smile in real life.

The thought of Ari is a happy one: dark hair, dark eyes, white chef coat, perfect plates. The Lula feels like a fantasy. I ask, *Do you keep in touch with anyone else?* I'm thinking of my former wine bar colleagues, thinking of Kati with her shampoo-commercial hair, and how she made sure to work as close as she could to him, maybe brush against his muscly arms.

No, he says. *Only you.*

Every few days, Ari and I say hi. I tell him about LA and the endless sunshine and the forest fires in the distance. I tell him about work, the perfect Sazerac, the laps around the dining room, the strange idea of the people in charge that their restaurant is world-class. He tells me about Per Se, how much he respects and fears the sous chef, prepping the famous oysters and pearls.

The management trainees have a job to do two times a day, three if we're feeling ambitious. That is to take the temperature of nearly every single ingredient in the restaurant. It's for reasons of food safety and compliance. If a customer gets sick and decides to sue us for poisoning him with infected filet mignon, we can look back for days, months, years and say we kept our filet mignon at a perfectly safe temperature. We have a machine that looks like a giant nineties-era cell phone, with a thermometer attached to a wire that pokes into dozens of ingredients and records what it finds. Chicken thighs: 37 degrees. Chicken livers: 36. If we find anything approaching 40, the danger zone where bacteria begin to zestfully multiply, we are to notify the kitchen manager, who is supposed to cool down the walk-ins with his mechanical prowess or massive quantities of ice, but who instead tells us to fuck off.

That they call him the kitchen manager and not the chef says a lot about the place. All of the recipes come from a big book and a TV-sized flat screen. They have been developed and perfected and qua-druple tested. There is no room for imagination here in the Pasadena kitchen. When it says add a pound of shredded cheddar, we measure. We execute.

The kitchen manager's job is to manage the inventories of the slabs of red tuna and the racks of ribs. The buckets of ears of corn and the jugs of liquid smoke. To make sure that when the book says eight ounces, the cooks add eight ounces, not eight and a half. And to make sure the refrigerator is colder than 40 degrees and the freezer is colder than 0 degrees and that these temperatures should be recorded twice daily in perpetuity.

On Saturdays, they gather us for management classes. If Saturday is a day off—it rarely is—we go to the class anyway. The three of us join the management trainees working in restaurants elsewhere in the LA area: Century City and Manhattan Beach and Santa Monica. Everyone is young and bleary with exhaustion. We conduct mock interviews (sample conundrum: the potential employee is qualified and sharp, but he is wearing flip-flops!) and climb on the roof to learn about HVAC systems, the So Cal air dry and hot. We make endless P&L reports and take tests on liquor laws, discrimination, harassment.

One time, I am late to class, stuck in a hellhole of LA traffic that doesn't move as far as I can see. I call the regional manager who teaches the classes and is more important than TJ, the GM, my boss.

"I'm so sorry," I tell him. "I've left extra time but I'm not moving at all. I'm going to be late."

"Welcome to LA," he says and hangs up.

When I get there, he's mid–inventory lecture. Something about whether to make a purchase in December and January, accounting stuff. He doesn't say anything and neither do I.

My head still rings with stress on my drive back to my restaurant in Pasadena. I scratch my Beetle in the parking lot, pulling into one of the faraway spots reserved for us. I get out and touch its peeling scar.

I throw on my suit jacket, head into work, past the koi.

"Can you do a temp sweep?" the kitchen manager asks, and I oblige.

I'm in the walk-in fridge, shivering, recording that the salad greens are a-okay when the GM says, "Hannah, step into my office."

He does have an actual office that he shares with the accountant and his other managers, but by his "office" he means his favorite booth. It's symbolic—he lives and breathes the dining room. His pulse is the pulse of the restaurant.

I slide in, the leather under me shiny and sticky. He runs his finger everywhere, checking for immaculateness.

"You were late today."

"I came straight here after class."

"You were late to class."

"I was crazy late! The traffic was hideous. I called and let them know."

"You should have called me."

"I'm sorry, I didn't think to call you."

"You made me look bad."

It becomes increasingly clear that TJ hates me. When I say "Good morning," he turns away. When I walk into the restaurant for my opening shift at 6:03 AM—the shift starts at 6 AM—he invites me back to his office, the booth.

"You're late."

I know I will have plenty of time to complete the opening tasks. The three minutes were three minutes lying in bed, listening to my head screech. I am trying to see this job as an adventure, an opportunity, but each day seems to drain me completely. I feel empty. I can't remember why I love restaurants.

"I'm sorry," I tell TJ. His bald head reflects the early morning light, the sun waking up out the window.

"As a manager, you are supposed to set an example. I should be having this conversation with our employees, not you." His hands are folded before me. His watch reads 6:05. Tick tick tick. The day ahead here feels like a prison.

My week of hosting is a weird sort of déjà vu, although we use paper and pencil, not OpenTable, which I am used to. The reservation books are marked up with the smudge of erasures from rescheduled tables, cancellations. With the exception of a girl named Becka, the hostesses—all hostesses, no men—are as cold to me as the walk-in freezer. But Becka chats with me at the hostess stand, tells me about her side business making jewelry. She's just got a great contract with a chain store, and she'll be up all night after work attaching clasps.

On Friday and Saturday nights, the crowd of people waiting for a table grows and grows, heaves and growls, pushes up past the koi. "Do you know who I am?" someone invariably asks, and I try not to giggle. Who are these people? The hostesses here wield their power with calm ferocity. "No," they say. "And it's beside the point right now. We will have a table ready in about thirty minutes. You are welcome to get a drink at the bar while you wait." The bar is three, four people deep. The bartenders pour and shake and run, run, run. In a few hours, their black uniforms will be bluish with damp and the floor full of straws and spills, a battlefield of detritus.

My favorite position by far is expediting, especially when it is busy. Expediting, I am at the helm of the restaurant, the captain of the great ship of service, flying through the sea of the night.

Adrenaline flies like crazy, the time goes by in a whirl. I bellow "Hands!" as the cooks snap endless plates into the pass. I anoint dishes with a grind of pepper, a drizzle of olive oil, a sprinkle of sea salt. "Pick up, pick up, I need hands!" I direct the servers to table 8, table 66, bar 7. "Hands!" Running food comes first, always first, and during the height of dinner rush we need a constant slew of servers. (This is why, at fine dining restaurants, there are runners.)

I have a great coach, a dapper older manager, who sets out to teach me how to expedite. Everyone must wear kitchen clogs, even TJ, but this guy somehow gets away with wingtips, doesn't even slip on the kitchen floor, slithery with dish soap, grease, and bleach.

"The expediter is in charge of the kitchen. That's you. And the kitchen needs clarity, order, precision to work." He doesn't leave my side. "Louder," he tells me. "There is no such thing as too loud." His advice—be more confident, know everything going on, set the pace, be relentless—is always right.

He stands next to me at the pass, showing me how to pull each ticket when it spits out of the machine, fold it in half, arrange it so the cooks can see the table number and I can keep track of time. Appetizers should arrive in three to five minutes; entrées in ten at lunchtime, twelve at dinner. We have our own dialect. An "H Rib" is the Hawaiian rib eye—it's slick with a pineapple juice, soy sauce, sesame and ginger marinade, which caramelizes over the flames, and really good. A "P Rib" is a prime rib eye. "Yo" is mayo. A "Pot E" is a baked potato, loaded with everything. I yell out the lingo until my throat is raw.

In Pasadena my eating disorder becomes a sort of soundtrack to my life. Often it fades quietly into the background. I'm too busy to binge or to spend a whole afternoon on the elliptical. Then just when I've forgotten about it—begun to think maybe this is something I'm over, something from the past, a bad dream—there's a sudden crescendo, a binge that keeps me up all night so that I'm still queasy at work the next day, my black suit gouging my waist. I skip breakfast. I skip lunch. I vow to only eat veggies and yogurt, the kind without sugar or fat or joy. I eat a whole enormous cucumber for dinner. I become so ravenous I do it all again.

"You're so healthy," Liz says when I pick at a salad I've concocted one rare slow Tuesday—all the veggies, a shake of Cajun seasoning, no dressing.

"No I'm not," I tell her. Liz is tiny and I wonder, eyeing the cheeseburger on her plate, if she could possibly understand.

"It was supposed to be a compliment," she says. "Anyway, this burger hits the spot." Liz's lunch smells like manna. I go back to work without finishing my salad.

Josh calls. He is in town from New York to meet with producers about a TV show. He is staying in Hollywood and eating excessively, as is his way.

"Come have a meatball with me."

After an opening shift, I drive to Dan Tana's. I tell Josh about my LA life. We share spaghetti and meatballs and veal scaloppini. The bread rolls are hot and fluffy and Josh fills his with butter. Sitting on crimson banquettes, below chianti bottles dangling from the ceiling, he tells it to me straight:

"Hannahleh, get out of there before it obliterates your soul." Hearing this fills me with relief. "Go write. Live in a small city, like Seattle or Austin or something. Write. Be young and poor. Get a weird job. Write some more. Corporate steakland is not for you."

He is right, of course. His certainty gives me courage.

"There's something else I wanted to tell you." We're finished with our meal and are walking down Melrose.

"I'm getting married."

"What?"

"To someone twice as old as you because I am twice as old as you."

"To who?"

"To Danit." Danit is Josh's friend. She is smart and pretty and it makes perfect sense. "The fact is that we are still in each other's lives and will be for many, many years." This time I know he is right.

Josh kisses me on the mouth, his hand on my back, outside the restaurant. "I have to go," I tell him, and I go. On the drive back to Pasadena I am happy for Josh. I feel a little less alone.

In New York, I loved being around wonderful food and wine, the revolving cast of fascinating and sometimes awful people, the perpetual motion, the obscene laughter, the camaraderie, the smell of clean dishes and buttery gougères baking, the soreness in my calves, the invites to someone's new speakeasy. I loved restaurants. I learn something here: I don't love all restaurants; I have no love for this one.

Hostess Becka returns from two weeks away at a jewelry conference. I am happy to see her smile back at the host stand. She sees me and opens her arms for a hug. I hug her back, then return to taking the temperature of trout.

An hour later, I'm sitting across the booth from TJ again.

"I heard you aced the sexual harassment test."

Oh lord. "Yup."

"What are the rules about inappropriate contact with employees?"

"Um, to not have any."

"So you should know better."

"I'm not sure what you're referring to."

I think that TJ must be joking. His lips contract into a frown; he is serious. He reprimands me for Becka, our hug. I can't imagine that two consenting adults are forbidden from a platonic embrace, but apparently, it's verboten for a manager to hug an employee. As a manager, I could get sued big time for sexual harassment or be responsible for a big restaurant lawsuit. Really?

It's serious enough to warrant a call up TJ's chain of command to the national office, an official slip of paper. I want to laugh and also to scream.

"Hannah, I'm afraid this is three strikes. The lateness to work. The lateness to your class without even so much as the courtesy of a call. You have to change your ways or you'll never make it here."

I can't imagine making it here, being TJ, doling out scoldings and spritzes of hair spray. I always have stubborn flyaways. The hair spray smells like DEET, makes my eyes water. A robot would be better suited to do my job.

I wonder if TJ has hated me from the get-go or if I have done something to offend him. He beams at Andras as if he is his own son and seems merely indifferent toward Liz. Maybe I remind him of his ex-wife, whom he talks about with such venom his eyes may pop out of his skull. Or maybe his contempt is a motivational tactic. If so, it's not working.

"You'll never be a good manager," he tells me.

"Then why am I here?" I ask, getting angry. My face is hot.

"Let's see if you can prove me wrong." But I only think of heading out the door and into my Beetle and driving all the way across the expanse of the country home to New York with my orange flower in front of me, windows down, endless possibilities. But I stay.

My mom plans a visit for New Year's. I take all of my scant vacation days. She flies to LA and we drive to Vegas, just because we have never been. Why not? Seeing her is like being home. Her hug floods me with relief. The road to Vegas is dusty dry and slow with never-ending traffic. We talk and talk.

We decide we will do one blowout meal. I research restaurants and choose one that seems fancy and fun. The chef is a serious chef. I wear a black dress with a low back, heels. My feet are calloused and perpetually unhappy, but my heart swells at being at a restaurant that is not a chain steakhouse, the candles twinkly, the room warm and smelling of browning butter. That magic.

I hit it off with the maître d'—"I work in the business, too"—and he pulls up a chair to chat with me and my mom after we have finished our dinner, pours us champagne, tells us where else to eat in Vegas, what it's like living here, until we are the only ones left in the dining room. He leaves his number with the check.

The next day is New Year's Eve. My mom has a weird, awful rash all over her legs; they won't stop itching. After we eat fluffy omelets in a neon diner, she needs to go back to our hotel room and slather on lotion. We both get under the alabaster sheets of our adjacent beds, turn on the TV. I text the maître d'. He texts back in seconds:

After service tonight we're all going to a rooftop to watch the fireworks. Join us?

I ask my mom if she minds. She says to go for it.

I head back to the restaurant, which is still busy. He says to the bartender, "Pour her a drink," and to me, "I won't be long." I sit at the bar, drinking more champagne. My feet hurt in my heels but the rest of me is light with possibility.

"Let's get out of here," he says as he emerges from the back. We head to someone else's bar, where everything is purple, velvet, and dark. The maître d' introduces me to his friends who run restaurants, chefs and managers and sommeliers, and I feel at home in a way I haven't felt since I flew to LA. These are my people: smart, funny, sarcastic, weird. I tell them about my job, TJ's cruelty, my criminal hug. They laugh.

The som has just sold a twenty-thousand-dollar bottle of wine to a celebrity, and so he buys champagne for everyone. In just a few minutes, it will be 2010. We are on the roof of someone's restaurant, and below us the city is savage with New Year's excitement.

"Move to Vegas," a lady chef says, her arms ragged with kitchen burns, her slinky shirt reflecting the lights on the Strip. "There are so many positions for restaurant managers. We need one now. You'd be a great fit. You don't need any hair spray and you can hug freely."

"That sounds perfect," I say. And on this night, as fizzy as our champagne, it really does. It is cheap to live in Vegas, I think, and I could be friends with this crew, manage a restaurant with an actual chef, save money, sip bubbles on rooftops.

At midnight, the sky fills with color and sound. I text my mom, my dad, Urs. The maître d' kisses me, a friendly kiss, and everyone hugs.

The next day, my mom's legs are a little better. We get manis and pedis, walk around casinos, and share another meal. I don't stop talking about whether to quit or not to quit. I'm trying to decide. Both options fill me with hot dread. I feel resigned. I fear that if I stay, Josh's prediction will come true. My soul will be constricted and slicked down, like my hair, until, starved for breath, it deflates. Yet if I go, I will be a quitter, a failure at my first real grown-up job. Each option feels disappointing. I am no closer to knowing what I want to do with my life.

But I'm not sure what to do next, where to go. *What will I do?* In the light of day, I don't think I can move to Vegas. The maître d' texts to say he's working all day, it was nice to meet me, and he hopes my job gets better.

On the drive home to Pasadena, there is hardly any traffic, and we fly through the desert. There is nothing for me in LA. This job felt like such an elegant answer to the nagging question of how to find a career, and now the question has returned, more forcefully, unanswered. I feel desolate as the desert.

I drive my mom to LAX and cry like a child when she leaves.

My phone rings on the car ride home. It is HR.

"Hannah, we have great news. We have your next assignment. You'll be moving to Nashville to manage the restaurant there." I have never been to Nashville. The thought of moving again to a city far away for a job that I hate chokes me. I don't know what to say, so I manage a "thank you" and hang up. I don't sleep that night.

I think TJ will be relieved when I give my notice, but he seems indifferent. I hand him my keys. He shakes my hand. The dapper older manager gives me a hug right in the middle of the dining room, and I wonder why he's allowed.

I call corporate to share the news. They tell me I have incredible potential and beg me to stay. "We can offer more money. Is it Nashville? We have other possibilities. Maybe Atlanta? Maybe Denver?" But I have made up my mind.

I finally understand that I don't just love the filling up of the reservation books, the theater of the tables turning and turning, the strawberries getting macerated and sides of meat seared, the deals done and proposals proposed. It's the creativity, the spirit, the heart. The feeling that anything can happen, because it can. Pouring a glass of sparkling Shiraz for your best friend's mom, changing some teenager's mind about blue cheese, creating a place for people to celebrate, to go out to, to come home to. The Corporate Steakhouse could never have been home. Walking out past the koi for the last time, I feel the vast freedom that comes from knowing this, from setting off to find the place that is.

I have another month until my lease ends, and I decide to stick around LA and do some soul searching. It's a wonderful month.

My fellow management trainees have graduated to bona fide manager status and have moved for assignments in San Francisco and Phoenix. No longer beholden to any rules, I ask the comedian bartender for coffee. He recounts Corporate Steakhouse stories that make me tear up with laughter, choke on my latte. When he says goodbye, I feel suddenly lonely. I buy two bars of chocolate and eat them in bed, covers up, TV on, novel in my lap. It works—I feel a little better.

TJ gave us training managers spa gift certificates for Christmas, and I book my massage, soak in a salty bath until my fingertips shrivel. I wander around LA, watching the colorful Venice crowds, taking off my shoes, feeling the sand in my toes and the ocean on my ankles. I take myself to the Getty Center and snap pictures of the views. I drink coffee with hipsters in Echo Park. I go to a comedy show with the comedian bartender and drink beers after. I spend a lot of time in the independent Pasadena bookstore, reading everything, piles of books in my lap, the afternoon becoming evening, which seems the most lavish luxury. I read self-help books and affirm nice things about myself even if I don't believe them. I write in my journal. I write poems. I write until my wrists hurt. At night, I prowl Craigslist, apply for jobs. I am alone but less often overcome with loneliness. I am somehow enjoying my own company. My freedom feels blissful. I make myself eggs, pasta with all the veggies. For the most part, I don't binge. I think, another move is coming, another chance to lose weight. Fresh starts are for diets. I will do it better this time. This time, everything will be different.

I call my mom a lot. She is a saint, listens to me obsess about what to do next, winding and unwinding the possibilities over the phone.

"Hey," she answers, when I ring her on one long Pasadena day. "I'm sitting at a bar with this woman, Margot. She and her husband own a restaurant in Philadelphia. It sounds pretty cool. She's looking for a manager. Want me to give her your number?"

Yes, yes, yes.

Margot calls the next day and tells me about her little restaurant with a big courtyard. The courtyard connects the spot to a boutique hotel, which she and her husband also own. It's a sprawling colonial brick home, built in 1787, gorgeous. They host a lot of weddings.

"Just drive down to Philadelphia when you get back to New York. It's easy. We can talk more about the job. And Kirk, my husband, is a developer. He always has apartments available. We'll line up a few for you to look at. Bring your mom!"

A job! An apartment! Bring your mom! It all sounds a little absurd.

"Great," I say. "I'm looking forward to it."

The comedian bartender comes to help me pack. I give him the thrift store office chairs, cleaning supplies, everything in my kitchen cabinets leftover from my binges. I try to give him my two plants, but he refuses, says he doesn't want the responsibility. I arrange for my Beetle to get shipped across the country, back to Hoboken. The plan is to stay with my parents for a while so I can plot my next move, maybe to Philly, maybe not. I am swimming in an ocean of possibility.

The man who picks up my car is a former Corporate Steakhouse employee. "I still have nightmares about that place. I'm glad you got out of there. Good luck with whatever's next." He gives me a hug. I am realizing that I am a hugger.

The comedian bartender drives me to the airport. I am dry-eyed. I am ready.

Agnolotti

New York is even more dazzling after missing it. I stay for a week. I talk all night with Urs. She's working in a biology lab at Columbia, studying the sounds frogs make. It's a little bit of science and a little bit of music, and at night she composes scores for string quartets, plays in a band where she wears a white full-body leotard. I go to see her band play. The room is nearly empty, but the event is being broadcast to South Korea, and there's a big screen where we can see a room packed with young people who have asymmetrical haircuts watching Urs do her thing. I am proud of her. The next day, we bring picnics to Riverside Park, shop at Beacon's Closet for floppy hats and flower-print dresses. Josh is thrilled for my freedom, takes me to Mile End for pastrami burgers.

"How's married life?" I ask.

"It's really good for me, Hannahleh," he says, and he seems happy.

The next day, I have a message on my phone: *A little birdie tells me you're in New York.* It's Ari.

We meet for ramen before his shift. He knows the ramen waitress and what to order. He has a million questions about the steakhouse. I have a million questions about Per Se.

"Don't be shy about slurping," he says, and sucks a fat noodle into his mouth. But I'm still shy about slurping.

When Ari says he has to go to work I walk him to the subway, the sidewalk slushy beneath our feet, sunlight bouncing off the gray snow, a tangle of knots like a challah braid in my stomach.

On Monday, my mom drives us to Philadelphia. I've never been on a job interview with my mom, before or since. The sky is leaden and gray.

We park in one of Kirk's buildings. It's as if it's my first day on the job. Margot greets us with big hugs. She introduces me to her and Kirk's partner, Vinny. When Vinny is not doing real estate deals with Kirk, he plays small roles in mob movies. He looks like a mafia guy, talks with all the bluster. My mom and Vinny chat while Margot gives me a tour of the hotel and the adjoining Elle Restaurant. The place is run-down and also beautiful—oil portraits of old men and grand ladies, French doors, and elaborate moldings. There's a dining room where tea is served, a tower of sugar cookies under a glass cloche.

Across the courtyard, the restaurant is small and dark with a tall wooden bar at the front. Tables in two rows fill the dining room, covered in eggshell linens. The kitchen is tiny, and we have to walk through an outdoor patio to get to the walk-in.

"Can I look inside?" A walk-in speaks volumes about a restaurant. There are boxes of produce stacked haphazardly, unlabeled trays of ravioli. Nobody has taken the temperature in here in a long time. This is the anti–Corporate Steakhouse.

Next, apartments. Margot shows me a whole floor of a narrow brownstone on a cobblestoned street, but the place I fall in love with is an airy apartment in a tall new building. Margot and Kirk own the whole thing. The doorman gives Margot a hug when we head up to see it. The bedroom is lofted above the kitchen, the living room ceiling goes up and up. Outside the windows, Philly presents itself as if in a painting. I can see William Penn atop Philadelphia City Hall, miniature people, miniature traffic. It's a four-block walk to my future work. I try to play it cool, but the apartment has me.

Next, Margot takes us to her studio. The floors and walls are draped in white fabric. Margot was a big-deal professional ballerina. I can see Margot as a ballerina—decades later, her spine is as straight as the columns in her buildings, her limbs so thin they seem dangerously fragile, like they may snap at any moment. A terrible illness ended her dance career. Margot found a new passion: photographing dancers. When she's not overseeing the restaurant, she runs a photo business. The lobby of my future apartment building is lined with her portraits, twirling women with impossibly long legs, men leaping, midair, their skin gleaming. "I'd like to take pictures of you some time," Margot tells me, examining my face. I wonder what she sees there.

Margot wants to take my mom and me to a new seafood BYOB for dinner before we head back to Hoboken, but I want to eat at the restaurant where I may be working to scope it out. The more information, the better. The food is American Italianish: bruschetta, caprese, pesto pasta, steak. It's mediocre. There's a ring of oil separating from my pesto. The bread is kind of stale, my wine glass chipped. Midmeal, Margot gets up to help bus plates from an adjacent table. All of this both worries and entices me—a challenge.

On the way home, the sky looses a wintry mix of sleet and rain, snow and frozen mess. My mom is nervous behind the wheel. "Is it weird that Margot didn't want to eat at her own restaurant?" my mom asks, but I understand wanting a change of scenery.

Can I see you tonight? Ari texts the next morning. I am reading about Josh's wedding in the papers and food blogs, about all of the celebrity chefs who cooked incredible dishes. I do not want to be married to Josh, but I want a big party with ridiculous food and sparkling cocktails and all the people I love.

Ari and I meet after his shift at Per Se. It's way past my bedtime when I make my way to Whiskey Traders in midtown, an after-work favorite for cooks, and my eyes feel heavy. The place is empty besides a few restaurant people, some loud Russian tourists doing shots.

We drink beers slowly, lean close together to hear each other's stories over the music. I watch his seriousness crack, a joke, the light shine through, and it makes my knees a little shaky under the bar. We sing along to the radio. We laugh. It's our second date.

"There's something I need to show you," he says, the gravity back.

"Show me!"

We leave our beers. The not-so-freezing February night carries the promise of spring, of possibility. For the first time in ages, I don't need my fuzzy hat. We walk outside to Robert Indiana's pop art *LOVE* sculpture, red and smiling on 55th Street, his hand in mine. It feels like a giant's hand, the weight of it. A homeless man jingles a cup, a siren whirrs, teenagers shriek, but midtown dims around us, disappears.

Four red, giant letters. His hand, strong. This feels like the heartbeat of this city, here, now, crappy bar, red street art, his smile, my smile.

"Look inside."

Wedged in the sculpture's *V*, chest height, is a letter, rolled up into a cylinder, like a joint.

"This?"

"Open it," and so I unroll the paper.

Hannah Chamuda, I'm so glad I met you. You are something special, it says in his loopy scrawl. And then he kisses me, soft lips, our bodies touching over winter coats, his hand in my hair, and everything is LOVE in shiny red plastic and invocation.

Our relationship begins with a kiss to end all kisses. There are fireworks and the earth shakes a little. All subway ride home, the lights blur, my heart whizzes down the dirty subway tracks.

There are different kinds of chefs. Chefs who cook from their heart. They make things with walloping flavors. I am not a chef, although I once wanted to be, but I like to think I cook this way. Ballsy, unbridled. I spent so much time not eating. When I do eat, I want it to be satisfying.

Then there is Ari. Ari is obsessively gentle, deliberate with food. He would never think of eating a Nutella, banana, and fluffernutter sandwich. Serious chefs are apt to sneer at vegetarians, to regard them with a pure and fiery hatred. Ari is the rare vegetarian and serious chef. Profoundly serious.

And so, our third date: Ari invites me to his apartment in Forest Hills to make dinner. I bring Barolo and DJ his stereo.

I haven't eaten all day in anticipation. My jeans are tight, the waistband like angry fingers digging into flesh I wish hard I could obliterate. I make these bargains with myself constantly, obsessively. Don't eat today and you can enjoy this meal tonight. And then, I break my own promises, my own heart.

I ask if I can help cook.

"No," he says. "I got it," his laser focus directed at the cutting board.

The agnolotti he makes for us are stunning, precise: military-neat rows of dough filled with sweet San Marzanos. I watch him as he pinches the eggy pasta off into identical satchels, twisting the ends. His fingers are long; his body is long. I would need a submarine, I think, to dive into the deep space behind his eyes.

He sees I am interested. "Do you want to make some?"

"Definitely!"

But I don't have a practiced hand. My pasta envelopes are lumpy and uneven. Like me, I think. He throws my batch into the trash unceremoniously.

He isn't mean about it or anything. We are falling in love. We eat them—slowly, slowly—talk and talk, make love for the first time—it is so slow I wonder if it will happen—talk more, smoke a joint, feed each other ice cream. (I am afraid to eat ice cream, it is not part of the bargain, but I eat from Ari's spoon, the cold rushing to my brain.)

I am wildly happy, but a small part of me mourns for my inferior, banished little agnolotti. They were rustic. They would have tasted good.

I decide to take the job in Philadelphia. Why not? A job and an apartment in a new city, a little package with my name on it, tied in a bow. I ask Margot if we can hire a new chef. She says it's already in the plans, the old one's heart isn't in it. I ask her for the title of general manager and the authority that entails to run the restaurant, manage the staff. She says of course. I ask her for ten thousand dollars more a year than I made at the steakhouse. She says no, but she can take two hundred dollars a month off my rent and throw in a free parking space in the apartment building's dark garage. "Plus, your money goes a longer way in Philadelphia." I say yes. There is no contract. I am twenty-two.

It's only after my first service that I think, *What have I gotten myself into?*

I am to take home all the cash each night after closing, deposit it in the bank the next morning. "Here," Margot shows me, handing me the keys to my new restaurant. "Hold the keys like this, so that they jingle, and then if anyone tries to rob you, you can stab them with the pointy part." Margot is the anti-TJ.

The chef is planning to open his own restaurant soon, and it's clear he does not particularly care about this one. He shows up after me, right before service, spends a lot of time smoking cigarettes on the balcony outside the walk-in or chatting with regulars at the bar.

I have ambitious plans. A menu that changes with the seasons. Desserts that don't come from giant cardboard boxes in the freezer. A point of sale system to track our sales. New wine glasses, sans chips. A waiter station that isn't full of old takeout menus and the chef's kid's old homework assignments.

The more questions I ask, the direr the situation appears.

"When was the last time we did inventory?"

"Uh, inventory?"

There are fruit flies swarming the liquor bottles. "When was the last time we deep cleaned the bar?"

In response, a blank stare.

I am fucked.

Ari calls at night, asks questions about the restaurant, my life, what do I love, what do I worry about, and we talk until keeping my eyes open is unbearable. He writes me real letters, sends them in the mail. On paper, his English is fragmented and stilted, but I can nearly hear his honey-coated voice, and I save every note.

I get into a routine. I join the gym across the street, which is so cheap it's nearly free, work out before work, walk to Whole Foods for a salad, walk to work, do paperwork at the bar while eating my salad, work, work, work, walk home with my keys at the ready the way Margot showed me, collapse on my sofa, call Ari, try not to fall asleep to his voice, which sounds like a lullaby. On Tuesdays and Fridays, I wait on line at the bank to deposit a rubber pouch full of cash. Mondays, the restaurant is closed and I explore Philadelphia, wandering around the

Italian Market, Reading Terminal Market, the cobblestoned streets of Old City. I sit in the Barnes & Noble in Rittenhouse Square, reading until closing time.

I am neither skinny nor fat, but I'm always trying for, thinking about, skinnier. Hence all the salads and working out. For a whole month, I don't binge. I wonder if it's something in the air in Philly, if it's Ari.

Ari and I get into a fight over the phone. He wants to visit me in Philadelphia, but I'm overwhelmed by the mess at the restaurant, the multitude of messes, the million things I want to get done. I'm also doing some freelance writing on the side, and when I'm not training staff and scrubbing the bar and counting our cash on Excel spreadsheets, deadlines abound. I ask if he could maybe come later, in another week or two. He hangs up the phone. He is hurt.

My mom gives me good advice: "If he's going to be your boyfriend, he's going to be around during the mellow times and the busy times. He's going to be part of your life, not separate from it. It's okay that you're busy. See if he can support you through everything that's going on."

I call and apologize. I meet him at the bus stop the next day.

It's our fourth date. Ari moves in. He quits his job at Per Se. "I've learned what I had to learn," he tells me. "I want to be with you."

I am giddy and dizzy. I've never had a real boyfriend before. I can't believe that this model-gorgeous man wants to be exactly that. I think of the life we will have, the tremendous meals, the profound sex, the amazing conversations late into the night. I imagine that with him I won't be lonely.

We take the Beetle back to Forest Hills to collect his stuff, of which there is little: beautiful plates, cast iron pans. I am twenty-two and ashamed by the fact that he is my first real boyfriend, by Corey, by Josh. I have never had a normal relationship with someone of an appropriate age. Ari wants to be an actual boyfriend. I am confused and astounded and thrilled as we drive down 95. "Empire State of Mind" is on the radio. My life with him sparkles with possibility.

I pay rent, and he cleans the apartment, rolling up his jeans to bleach the bathroom until it shimmers, the muscles flexing in his arms. He hangs a single light from an exposed pipe. It turns the city twinkly. I am freelancing, too, after work, before work, whenever I can squeeze in some minutes. I write a profile of Stephen Starr, the Philadelphia restaurateur who seems to own half the spots and all of the hype in my new city. After our interview he invites me to dinner at Butcher & Singer, his swanky steakhouse. I bring Ari, wear a red dress; we get a corner table and eat with our legs touching, our hips touching, lamb chops, red wine that makes me pucker. I'm tipsy when I have an idea.

I give Ari Starr's number. They hit it off. Turns out Starr has a soft spot for Israelis.

Soon Ari has a job as sous chef at Parc, Starr's French bistro in Rittenhouse Square, which I think of as a Balthazar wannabe. Now Ari can contribute to rent. Sometimes he brings home quart containers of granola, tiny brioches swirled with cinnamon. We both work crazy restaurant hours and rarely see each other. I have Mondays off. Ari, Thursdays. Sometimes I go to Parc on Mondays, alone or with friends, sit at the bar, drink bubbly. Their roast chicken is no joke, the juices dripping onto a pile of *pommes purée* soft as butter.

On Thursdays, Ari comes to my restaurant, chats with Margot. "This place has so much potential," he tells her.

One day Margot comes by my apartment, our apartment now, to deliver some paperwork. It's Monday and Ari is not working until the late shift, so he's home whipping meringue to fold into his *pain perdu* with the first of the summer raspberries for breakfast, which he will spend so long cooking it is brunch, then lunch. Margot is so impressed she asks him to be the chef at Elle Restaurant.

We talk about it for mere minutes until we decide, of course, it's too great of an opportunity to pass up. We'll run a restaurant together; it will be practice for our own place. A dream.

Ari is striking, tall, thin but impeccably muscled. He speaks in a syrupy Israeli accent. On the streets of Philadelphia, model scouts press their business cards into his big palm. Sometimes they tell me, "You're pretty, too." But I know he is the pretty one. Surreally pretty. I catch myself staring: his sharp jaw, his cheekbones, his underwater eyes. That he likes me, loves me, seems unfathomable.

Every so often in old books, wedged in my journals, I find his love letters. *My dearest Chamuda, you have my heart forever. You are the sun.* Ari speaks in hyperbole. He means every word.

At the start of life with Ari, there are painstakingly elaborate feasts. Ari has started to eat fish, too, if it's wild and up to his exacting standards. I come home to salmon tartare with sesame and hot oil, a whole plate of sushi art, rices and seaweeds and fish in complicated compositions. The best paella I ever imagined. Fat strands of pappardelle hanging from the kitchen cabinets, drying. He prepares breakfast for hours, whipping meringue to fold into buckwheat pancakes or fashioning custard for Marcona almond and apricot pain perdu.

There are risottos and veggies and pancakes that would embarrass a perfectly decent cook. They are good, almost too good, freakishly good. They make me giggle with unbridled delight.

I am terrified of getting fat. Afraid I am already fat and he is too polite to tell me. I haven't weighed myself in years now, petrified of what the scale might say. Still, I feast. The almond macarons he leaves me on our countertop taste of clouds and of joy and of my own mind-numbing fear.

Ari runs his fingers down my spine. "You're the most beautiful woman in the world." But I shake my head in staunch dissent. He drags me to the mirror. My face looks like a cruel joke next to his model face. "Look!" he says, but I cry, and my hot tears fall on his perfect chest. He shakes me. "Wake up, Hannah Chamuda." Our apartment spins. Outside Philadelphia spins, the whole world spins, and it makes me nauseous.

Ari and I embark on relaunching Elle Restaurant. Always, I wanted my own restaurant. Here is our chance. We're in bad need of a new executive chef, a new menu, a facelift. It is a chance to bring his vision to life. Or our vision.

On a Saturday night at the end of July, the departing chef cooks his last pasta with basil pesto and grilled chicken.

We have until Monday at 7:30 in the evening, when Ari will present a tasting menu to the owners and eighteen of their closest friends. We have a long wooden table set up in the garden. Everything is green and blossoming as if awaiting his banquet. Tuesday night, Elle will open for dinner like any other night.

Saturday, after dinner service, we stay late to clean. Ari starts cooking stocks in giant pots and organizes the kitchen that is still scattered with gorgonzola, truffle oil, and chicken breast—all of these things will be gone in no time. I chop carrots, onion, and garlic until my fingers go tingly.

Ari begins what is to be the first of many, many days with a measly modicum of sleep and food. He is working, working, working. His only breaks are for quick puffs of cigarettes out back.

It is my job to plan the tasting. I decorate the long table with pots of sunflowers. We have agreed on twenty guests. The problem: not everyone has RSVP'd. And the owners bring more friends than I knew about. At least twenty-two people are expecting dinner.

Ari is angry, his voice low and impatient. "We planned for twenty. We will have dinner for twenty."

"Can we just make slightly smaller portions?"

"No," is his answer.

"These are Margot and Kirk's friends. Margot and Kirk are our bosses. We have to make something work," I plead.

"We do not. We agreed. Twenty."

It's our first night working together and already I wonder if we have made a terrible mistake. I'm in the bathroom trying not to cry when my phone rings. It's Margot. She's so sorry, one of her guests, a couple, can't make it. Thank God.

"Ari." I head back into the kitchen, which is buried in steam and smoke and clatter. "Twenty it is."

The meal is astronomical. Cold beet "borscht" salad: tapioca infused with beet, whipped horseradish yogurt, sweet roasted beet, crispy Parmesan, and a small mound of herbs. Pan-roasted corn ravioli with corn crème fraîche, pickled corn, and caramelized corn puree. Diver scallop "islands" in a sea of clam consommé. Long Island duck breast with our own duck sausage and brined cherries. Braised and glazed short ribs with bacon melba and tarbais bean puree.

"Your boyfriend is a genius," the guests say. And "It's the best meal we've ever had. And we've traveled the world. And we're nearing sixty. And this tops them all." I am proud. It's hard work for me, too, training the staff who are used to serving mushy pasta, getting ten courses of silverware on the table when we have not nearly enough forks and knives, wine pairing, linens, allergies. Tomorrow we'll be back here, doing it all again.

"Can I take your photos?" Margot asks me every so often, after a P&L meeting with our accountant or while I'm taking bar inventory, counting bottles with the bartender. "Your pictures will be striking."

Finally, I assent. I have always hated the way I look in photos, ungraceful and bulky and shiny-foreheaded. I've seen Margot's portraits of grinning schoolkids and professional actors and they are gorgeous. Maybe she will help me see myself through kinder eyes. Before work one day, I blow out my hair and line my eyes with black liner. I wear a black dress and boots and fill a tote bag with some other wardrobe options.

I walk the few blocks to her studio. It's a sunny day, so we decide to take some photos around Philly. When the traffic slows, she directs me into the middle of Walnut Street and snaps and says to move my hip forward and snaps and tells me to sit cross-legged against a Curtis Center building and snaps again. "Let's do some in jeans," she suggests, back in her studio. I change while she is adjusting her tripod. "Flip your hair, it's getting a little flat." I sit on a chair in front of a white wall and stack one ankle on my other ankle. I feel silly, but I tell myself feeling silly is part of the process. "You're doing great," Margot reassures me. "Don't be afraid to look at the camera like you mean it. There you go! Like that. You're a natural."

At work, I stuff the bag of clothes and shoes under my desk. It's a busy night today—we have a graduation dinner, and the garden will be full of Philadelphians eager to feel spring air on their faces, drink a happy hour glass of pinot blanc, watch the daffodils open their sunshine petals.

As Ari works more and more, he cooks at home less and less. The pasta maker, once a trusty companion, languishes in the closet. I understand. I am tired, too. By nighttime, my back aches. We go shopping for good shoes.

At home, Ari cleans the whole apartment, a scrub brush in one hand and a bottle of bleach in the other. I open the windows to let out the chemically smell, which he in turn shuts. "Philadelphia is dirty," he explains. I go for a walk to get some groceries and escape the ferric air.

Back at home, I find him lying comatose on the couch. Without his shirt, he looks bony, all ribs and hair. There's a documentary about his favorite Italian chef on TV but he's not watching it. I try to rub his back; he pushes me away. His eyes are hazy.

"Are you okay?"

"Am I okay? What does that even mean?"

"I'm worried about you."

"I'm sure you have other things to worry about."

"You're the most important thing." At that moment, I mean it. I want nothing more than for him to be happy—for us to be happy.

"The apartment was disgusting."

"Thank you for cleaning."

"How can you live like that, in filth?" The apartment wasn't close to filthy. Now, it nearly sparkles. I think, *I could scream*, but there seems to be no use trying to have a fight with Ari. I leave him on the couch and curl up in bed with a book and a pint of frozen yogurt. Sometime in the middle of night, I feel him sink into the bed beside me. "I'm sorry," I think I hear him whisper into my neck. But in the morning, I wonder if I dreamt it.

I have worked at restaurants before, but now I am in charge. I stay up after work making a playlist, but Margot hates my playlist so we're back to slow jazz. A server calls in sick. There is money missing from the cash register. A molding is coming loose from the wall. The printer has lost the evening's menus. A regular refuses to tip. Ari is fighting with a server. There is always something and something else, and I count the days 'til Monday.

Ari loves with the fibers of his toes and eyelids, with each breath and all his gigantic, hurting heart. He works the same way. Fiercely, tirelessly, wildly. He comes in early to order the country's most perfect zucchinis, which we find from a tiny farm in Ohio, and stays after his last cook and dishwasher have bleached the floor into a pearly shine. His twelve-hour days become fourteen-hour days, then sixteen. He stops eating, and our boss worries that Ari's pants are falling off his hips. When we visit his family in Jerusalem, his mom's face freezes in concern.

"Tell him to eat!" they both say to me. I hear the same words from our sous chef, our regulars. I tell him plenty. I bring him Frappuccinos, and they melt, forgotten. I carry slices of pizza to work in brown paper bags, sandwiches, old-fashioned donuts, which are his favorite.

He doesn't eat for so long that he gets lightheaded, needs to sit down. I understand. For the last few years, I have been starving and bingeing and bingeing and starving. I know how the world looks when I've been without real sustenance for days, blindingly bright and two-dimensional, the way it hurts to balance on my feet. I don't know what to do. I am too fucked up to help him. Ari's thinness makes me feel fat, round in comparison. On some days, it feels like a personal affront. Like he is winning at my expense.

Still, on Monday, our day off, we try the new restaurants that are popping up all over Philadelphia. We share crostini heavy with creamy porcini and drink foamy beers with our staff. We laugh until the beer comes back up our noses. He carries me, still laughing, down the street. We get a puppy, named Nuni, and go foraging for ramps: me, him, the shaggy dog. I think, *This is what I wanted, what I want.* We have sex on the kitchen counters, in the shower, on the roof deck until we hear a noise and cover ourselves. The laughter is like a drug. It will save me.

Ari's cooking is all cerebral. In a dish called "Tastes, Smells, and Touches from the Garden," the waiter punctures a plastic-wrapped plate to release "pine air." There are "rainbowed trout," a rainbow trout cloaked in a rainbow of paper-thin veggies: beets, carrots, squashes. It is showstopping.

Ari's cooks, his apostles, are all fiercely loyal to him, which is why they work for us for terrible money, come in as the sun rises to chiffonade and stay deep into the darkest night to mop the floors, cryovac kirsch-soaked cherries, leave fragrant veal stock at a whisper of a simmer.

Each night, when the last plates are whisked away, Ari and Jay and Evan and Cody crack open their beers and leave the stifling kitchen for the cool garden, smoking cigarettes, bullshitting, gathering a second wind for the relentlessly thorough cleanup Ari mandates.

"Can't they clean without you?" I ask every so often, my eyes blurry after the long days, the soles of my feet sore. After all, he is the chef, their leader. Most chefs gladly let their subordinates do the hard work of scrubbing, mopping, and washing. But it is important to Ari to work beside them. At night his soft skin smells of bleach.

Ari is up all night reading about savory ice cream texture and airy macaroons and tofu so rich with umami it might explode. In the mornings, he and his cooks bring these things to exquisite, intricate life. They dehydrate parsnips and turn gazpacho into popsicles and meat-glue short ribs into glossy towers.

I post all the Craigslist ads searching for Ari's cooks. They say something like:

> *Looking for a cook with a shit-ton of energy and passion. Helps if you are ambitious and hungry, obsessed with fine dining and serious technique, but willing to work for nearly nothing, peel fingerlings until your fingers go numb, scrub the fryer 'til it shines like the moon.*

Cooks come and go, don't show up for their shifts, throw plates across the garden and storm out, leaving their knives behind. Our pimply and kickass intern leaves us to go back to school for the semester. We interview so many people we forget who is who. I hand out W4s like candy.

Slowly we get Ari's crew together. They come and they actually stay. They move like dancers in the tiny kitchen. They know all the steps, they finish each other's sentences, fight with their hearts flung open, would fuck up someone for each other.

I like Jay the best, who has just graduated from college and talks way too fast. He is always reading, plotting, growing tomatoes in his little apartment that he shares with a million guys and is caked deep in filth. "It's a disgusting apartment," Ari complains. "But he grows some good tomatoes." We eat them like apples, make them into gel, and string them on ribbons of pappardelle.

Cody is tall, as if he has been stretched out, and tattooed, and he's always high, sometimes out of his mind. His eyes are painted with a permanent film of faraway. But he is a great cook—lightning fast, serious. Ari has to pick him up from jail one day while I watch over his kitchen. We lend him money for bail that we don't expect to be paid back.

Ari won't hire women. He tries once, at my urging—a blonde pastry chef with buff arms—and when she doesn't work out, he recommits to his strict no-girl stance.

"Ari," I tell him, "that is cruel. That is absurd."

"You don't understand," he says. I notice I am starting to hate this man I thought I loved.

And so he has his boys. And his boys love him and fear him.

One day I find Jay in the walk-in, crying.

"Are you okay?" I want to give him a hug, and I am no longer in the Corporate Steakhouse, so I do.

"Sort of," he says. "Chef is not happy." And when Chef is not happy, nobody is happy.

"Ari," I say, back in the kitchen. Ari's head is down. He's fiddling with his new sous vide machine. My arms are full of starched napkins. "Jay is really upset."

"So am I," Ari says, his eyes bloodshot with anger. He barely looks up.

So I stay out of it. I have my own staff to watch over. I have to make sure Jason isn't drinking all the beers in the basement, and Richard doesn't forget what an Espelette pepper is, and that Jules's creepy admirer, who sits at table 49 with a grin and a whiskey, stays as far as possible from Jules. We all need to fold a pile of napkins, or we'll run out in the middle of dinner rush.

In summer one day, Cody comes to work more fucked up than usual. It's not just his hands that shake, it's his whole tall body. Ari tells him to go home. Still, I worry for Cody that day, unsteady beneath the hotel pans stacked in his ropy arms.

Cody says, "I'm fine. I'm working. I'm staying." Ari needs him, and so he takes him out back and tells him this is the last time, has to be the last time. Ari and I go over the menu for the night: stinging nettle risotto, salmon belly ceviche, braised lamb shank.

I gather up my staff to discuss the new dishes: "The risotto is garnished with lovage, fried jasmine flowers, thyme confetti." They are getting good at this and I am proud of them. I have my people, too.

Cody, high on who knows what, fries up delicate, lovely jasmine flowers, lowering each into a big vat of oil with a slotted spoon. The oil bubbles and sizzles. He drops the spoon into the hot oil. His mind somewhere far away, Cody reaches in with his left arm to retrieve it, as if he is reaching into a sink for a bar of soap. This is no sink. This is oil at a ferocious bubble; Ari reminds his cooks the oil must be raging.

Cody screams so loud in shock we all run to the kitchen. He screams and screams. Ari calls 911. I turn on the tap in the big dishwashing sink and Cody's arm wheezes under the cold water. There are tears in his eyes. The paramedics are fast. Cody and Ari leave through the green garden in an ambulance, the skin red, missing from Cody's elbow to his fingertips, fried like the jasmine flowers.

We have two men down and a busy night ahead. I gather the staff. "Cody is in good hands." They look at me skeptically. "We need to focus tonight." I jump in to expedite, hitting up plates with tarragon oil and sunchoke chips and wisps of basil foam.

Two hours later, Ari is back. I want to give him a hug, but he won't even look me in the eye.

"How is Cody?"

"He'll be fine. They say they've seen worse burns."

"What about you? You okay?"

"We'll talk about it later." But we don't talk about it later. Instead we disappear into the hive of service. "Should I wait for you to go home?" I say when the register has been emptied, the numbers tallied, the tables wiped and set.

"Don't bother."

Our apartment feels too big without him. I'm exhausted but I cannot sleep, even when he curls himself beside me at some ungodly hour.

The next day, Cody is in the kitchen with a puffy bandage.

"I thought you were going to fire him," I say to Ari, who shrugs.

"He's a good cook. We need him." At Elle, whatever Ari says goes.

I'm jealous of how intensely and wholeheartedly Ari takes to his work. I love his food, I come to love the staff I hire and schedule and train and train and laugh with. But I'm not deeply satisfied like he is. Something is missing.

In search of this happiness, I decide to start a cheese program at Elle. Margot and Kirk find an antique hutch we can use as a cheese case, à la The Lula. Cheese is best served at room temperature when all the flavors come to life fully, but health code dictates otherwise. To get around this, we make a tiny sign in the cheese case: "For Display Only." A lie, of course.

I deck out my new case in straw mats, clean it as assiduously as Ari would. I shop for cheese at Di Bruno Brothers and at the Italian Market. I order wholesale from Murray's, and when the boxes of cheese arrive with my name on them, it's like Christmas. I study up on *The Cheese Primer* by Steven Jenkins, which I keep in my cabinet's single drawer. I teach my staff that goat cheese is frosty white because, unlike cows and sheep, goats convert beta carotene into colorless vitamin A. I give them tastes of azeitão and wait for them to be awakened as I was. When I have the time, I delight in turning on my tables to smoke-kissed Idiazabal, pineappley Challerhocker. Close your eyes, it's as if you're in the Alps where this beauty is made, the cold air smells of wild herbs.

We get a rave review, then another. A big part of me is proud. I gush to regulars, reporters. This whiz-kid chef, the genius, my boyfriend. And yet, he is different here. Who is this boy I love, throwing a glass at the bewildered dishwasher? Where is the joy in this, listening to Ari scream at the staff I trained with a patience I didn't know I had? Counting the register night after night? Folding mountains of starched off-white napkins?

I eat. I eat and eat.

His food, his food. Gougères, buttery and soft and cloudlike, swiped through fresh-churned butter infused with the smoke from burning hay. Peanut butter mousse and petits fours. Scraps from the short ribs, fatty and ethereal. Duck prosciutto we cure ourselves in the basement. Risotto laced with oxtail. Lobster poached in vanilla butter.

Ari gets thinner. His bones jut into my thighs as we fall asleep, hugging. I get fatter. My jeans rip between my thighs.

Still, Ari insists I am beautiful, I am perfect. But we stop sneaking off places to kiss and kiss and kiss. We stop having sex. We stop telling stories. We work together, we live together, and I miss him terribly. I miss the love-letter author, the cursive swirls of his imperfect, beautiful English. I miss the exuberant breakfast artist. I miss his adoration, his hands on my body, our shockwaves.

"I have something for you!" Margot says. She goes a week or two without stopping by the restaurant, then another week of hanging out every night, chatting with regulars and worrying that the music is too loud or not loud enough. I can never seem to get the music right.

"Here!" She hands me a few disks. "Your pictures came out beautifully. I gave you a few copies so maybe you can give them to your mom and dad, or just have them in case they come in handy."

For some reason I am nervous as I take the pictures from her hands. "Thank you so much, Margot."

I slip a disk into the computer in the tiny office I share in the hotel across the garden. Oh my god. Oh my god. I have to eject the disc immediately I am so mortified. I see a whale, a monster. My arms look like Ari's homemade sausages, overstuffed in puckering skin. The flesh of my belly folds over my jeans. I wish I could unsee these photos, take it all back. Why did Margot say I looked good when I look grotesque?

Since I have been no-longer-an-official-anorexic, I have not weighed myself. I know I weigh more than I used to, but I have no concept of how much. The pictures say to me: *way too much*. They say, *You have let yourself go*. They say, *You have failed*. I try not to cry. I'm at work. I slip the CDs into the trash. I cannot face the evidence of myself. I think, *I have dieted before successfully, I will diet again*. I will fix this. I will fix myself. It's only a question of not eating Ari's gougères and his pain perdu and mochas from Starbucks before work. More time at the gym. Saying no thank you. That rumbly stomach. Mustering all my strength. Here I go.

We're up at the time of the day when the city still yawns—the sky is mud dark, garbage trucks jangle along Locust Street, a single ambitious jogger has the sidewalk to himself.

I landed us a spot on the local morning news. Bill, the anchor, is one of our regulars. He sits at the bar most nights, ankles crossed, bow tie perfect. Bill drinks single malts, neat, maybe hits on an unlucky woman or tells whoever happens to be nearby, usually me, an awful joke: "Why do vegetarians give good head? Because they're used to eating nuts."

One night, I interrupt him. "Can we come on your show? Ari can cook something from our spring menu. His new dishes are stunning. We can talk about the restaurant. New chef. Girlfriend GM. The restaurant couple. We're a good local story."

"Why not?"

He slips me his card across our tall bar. The next day, I talk to his bubbly producer on the phone, and this morning we're here at an obscene hour with boxes of sunshine-colored zucchini flowers, pillowy ricotta, Ari's tear-inducing gougères. His food has a way of making people lose their cool.

I woke up an hour before to dig my blow-dryer out of our closet and attempt to do my hair. Still, it frizzes in the late Philadelphia spring, the morning drippy with humidity even before dawn. Ari zips up my new maroon dress, scooped neck, A-line skirt. I have to hold my breath a little to get it to close over my belly, my boobs. I think it will look good on TV, flattering, but for a moment the old fear takes away my breath like a sucker punch. The mirror taunts me—I am too fat for TV, screens will moan in protest throughout the homes of the Philadelphia metro area, shatter in airwave-transmitted disgust. My face gets hot with self-loathing, cheeks red.

I turn away from the mirror; take out Ari's chef's coat from our closet. I got it dry-cleaned for the occasion. Its crisp white makes his hair and eyes luminescent with dark. He is all cheekbones and deep-set eyes. He stuns.

With heels, I am nearly as tall as Ari. He holds my hand, tight, tense like he may otherwise bolt. Under his bright eyes are shadows, blue as the night sky.

I want him to tell me I look beautiful. I will settle for good, even. But he looks past me. I tell myself he is nervous, too.

"This is silly," he says for the millionth time. "I belong in the kitchen, not on TV."

"People will love you on TV, and then they'll come in droves to feast on the awesome things you make in the kitchen."

"Maybe," he concedes, but he is sullen.

At the network, the walls are white as new snow. They offer us coffee, unfurl the plastic wrap from a tray of pastries. But Ari's attention goes straight to the good plates we've brought from home. They're nicer than the plates at the restaurant, flecked with gold and featherweight enough to make me nervous.

Dropping one is the sort of move I imagine I would make, obliterating his masterpiece, shards of porcelain all over the floor, my hands bloody with shame.

But the plates make it, safe. "Where's the Manuka?" he barks, and I hand him the squeeze bottle of aureate honey.

Ari pipes ricotta into papery squash flowers, chiffonades basil into verdant wisps, his focus precise as the peaks and valleys he makes with two hands on the pastry bag. His hands are shaking, but his plate is perfect. All his plates are perfect.

"What's the plan?" I ask the producer. Her hair is big and she is tiny, her waist maybe the size of one of my thighs, if that. She wears a suit with a jacket super-cinched to show this off. I think her organs must be miniature to fit inside her pinprick body, like bird organs. "Ari's almost ready with his dish. Do they need to do our makeup?"

"When Ari finishes, he'll go for makeup. Then the next segment, then commercial break, and he's on. He can take his time with the food. The makeup will only take a minute."

"And mine?"

She keeps smiling but cocks her head, like she is talking to a confused child, a pet. "Bill's notes are for a cooking segment with Ari. There aren't any mentions of you. You can watch from right over here."

Suddenly, my dress feels unbearably tight around my body, like I may rip its whole length open with my next inhale. I am too big by about twenty pounds or several million. I am a monster of the most eye-shatteringly hideous variety. Even my heart, it beats too loud. Of course I am not welcome on Bill's show. It all makes sense. I am mad at the stupid show and mad at the world for what it asks of me and mad at myself for caring, for wanting what it wants, more than anything to look skinny in my dress. Again, I have let myself down.

Ari does better than I expect, even cracks a smile. His English is not amazing, but when he talks about the farm where we get our summer squash, the sheep's milk ricotta, his eyes shine so bright there could be fire. Bill fawns, in his news anchor sort of way.

"Are you French?"

"Israeli." When people can't identify his drippy vowels, they assume French.

When Bill takes a bite of Ari's food, his jaw relaxes, forehead uncreases.

"Damn," Bill says when the cameras stop rolling, "you can cook."

"You could have dinner some time," Ari retorts. "With your drinks."

After, Ari washes his face. We go for breakfast at the diner. I get an omelet, toast. Ari orders coffee. "I'm too nervous to eat." The steam blows up his chin. When he lifts it to sip, his hands tremble still.

"You were fantastic. Really! I am proud of you. You should be, too."

I am trying to play it cool, but my disappointment wraps itself around me, tighter than the dress. I had practiced my lines about the restaurant, our garden, meeting Ari, asking him to come work with me, our story. The dress, the hair, feel laden with stupidity. Ari is storybook gorgeous. He's going to be big someday, the heartthrob celebrity chef. Of course they didn't want me, dimming his sunshine: ordinary, chubby.

No one wants me to join Ari on TV because of the roundness of my belly, I am sure. It doesn't matter, the other stuff. I have failed in the biggest way.

I stop home before work to walk Nuni. I collapse on the couch and he curls up with his little head on my knee. I take off the dress, stuff it in the trash can.

Usually I am in the front of the house, greeting guests and running food, inquiring about Mr. Taffer's sister's health and the newest local artisanal tonic, turning up the music and turning it down again, polishing glassware in a pinch, and there is always a pinch, frothing milk for cappuccino, stepping to the back to make a cheese plate, talking the angry busboy off a ledge under the gray sky.

But one cook is in jail, and Cody is in the hospital, and Jay is MIA (did Ari make him cry for the last time?), and so here I am, next to Ari in the kitchen. At night, we hug in bed. He runs his long fingers through my hair, tickles the part of my tummy I hate. This week we work hard side by side, not touching but almost touching. We wear matching starched whites, crisp aprons. He ties mine around my waist: neat, tight. Jules takes my spot in the front of the house, posts the schedule on the clipboard, runs the show.

There is something zen about setting up for service in the morning. The front of the house is empty and clean—floorboards glimmer in the early sunlight, the bar waxed sleek. The kitchen is white and gleaming as the moon. Before the night's downpour of chaos, quiet envelops us.

Ari teaches me his meditation of preparation, *mise en place*, everything in its rightful spot. We start with black bags in the trash cans, yellow butter and kosher salt in nine pans by the stove, which is already kicking up its pilot light, eager to get to work. Squeeze bottles of gold-green Spanish olive oil, white balsamic, rice vinegar. Check the walk-in and the lowboy. Clipboards fat with sheets of inventory and prep and brainstorms, sketches of big plates full of swirls and scribbles, details and grandiosities.

The morning is about precision, order. Each purple carrot peeled to reveal its tangerine-hued interior. Parsley leaves pressed and dried into chips. Bing cherries pitted and left to macerate in kirsch. Quart containers full of brilliant colors and textures, polenta from summer corn, crème fraîche dotted with lime zest, pickled banana peppers. Everything labeled and dated, lined up in rows as neat as soldiers.

At night, the ferocity of service buzzes in our ears, swirls our thoughts into cyclones, keeps us running, sweating, high.

Here, Ari is chef. (The word *chef* derives from the Old French *chief*. It means head.) Ari's power is absolute. His army of cooks does precisely what he says. He demonstrates: This is how you mandolin summer squashes into translucent ribbons. This is how you squeeze ground lamb into a tube of sausage, fragrant with garam masala and ginger. This is how you fry fish skins until they crackle percussively.

This is my second day on the front lines in Elle Restaurant's back of the house, and I like it. There's alchemy. I slice yellow corn kernels off their cob, slit and open their cornskins, cook them low and slow with the stock that's been simmering all night, strain and strain again, fold in butter. It's the best polenta I've ever tasted—like the sweetest summer corn condensed. The texture is like ice cream; the color is sunshine.

And then. Service. Showtime. The servers, my servers, are aproned and ready to go. They've been briefed on the specials over family meal: pasta with Ari's melty tomato-eggplant sauce, Hudson Valley duck prosciutto with compressed peaches, agnolotti folded neatly around sweet peas and chèvre, chicken with sofrito and some sort of gigantic purplish heirloom bean.

The first plates snuggle up to the stovetop's flames that are all roaring now, the tickets rolling in. Tonight it's me and Ari on the line, plus James our dishwasher, who is jumping back and forth between the big sinks and the *garde manger* station—literally "food keeper," the person responsible for salads and cold apps, the dishes that don't involve cooking.

It's Ari and me in the heat. It's so hot our quart containers full of iced tea become warm tea in mere minutes; we are slick with sweat. The heat is barbaric, slowing our thoughts, pressing against our skin, our faces, relentless.

I start each dish—he cooks—I plate. Every dish gets his exacting eye before the waiters whisk it away, white towels folded over their arms, their eyes shiny with focus. "I need hands," we call and call again. The servers better come, and fast, or else. Ari's wrath cuts through the restaurant like knife blades sharpened to magnificent incisiveness.

Chicken breast, wrapped tight in its crispy skin, gets a sear in butter, as does the sausage we made earlier with the bird's dark meat. I pass him the little parcels of chicken from the lowboy, slice a knob of sausage from our thick links; he places them on the blazing pan. In the pan next door: the oblong beans, a clove of garlic, a sprig of oregano, a drizzle of ouzo.

When he says go, I move the chicken pieces onto a bed of sofrito—citron-colored from bell peppers and yellow tomatoes and Vidalia onion. I shake a spoonful of beans onto the plate in sort of a tadpole shape, precise but organic. On top, "confetti" made from carrots and cilantro rains down, because this plate is a celebration (and for texture and flavor). The higher I sprinkle confetti from, the more evenly it dots the plate, although it also leaves confetti all over the kitchen, a vegetal blanket, which I help James wipe down and mop up, again and again.

There are the other dishes, too, and Ari and I get into a rhythm. This is not a partnership. He says chop and I chop. He says move to the left and there I am, over to the left, by the pass. He says move faster and I don't see how, but I try, wiping the plates, confetti-ing the confetti, my cheeks hot, my hands moving before my brain quite catches up. Table 27, down. "I need hands. Hands!"

"You're not bad for a girl," Ari says, somewhere midrush, breaking the intensity of our concentration. Ari's sexism makes me cringe. But I'm proud, too, my bandana on my head, my focus like a razor. My agnolotti are not awful. My peaches taste of the setting sun.

Dinner rush peters out, slowly. The orders slow to a less manic pace. We're still in it, though, thick, James rushes to get us more plates, bowls. I run to the walk-in—really run—for more polenta. I retie my bandana. Short ribs. Chicken. Table 7 are vegans, and Ari makes them ribbons of fresh pasta with the rest of the zucchini, toasts hazelnuts, head down.

"Hannah," he says. "Take care of table 12."

Chicken, chicken, agnolotti.

"Yes, chef."

I do my thing, get the plates hot and ready, wipe the pan clean, and plop in a fist of butter, which has melted in the kitchen heat.

Next, to slice the sausage into a neat ring. My knife on its taut skin. And there is Ari, his head nearly touching mine, coming over to check on my progress.

My blade punctures the casing, but instead of creating a smooth slit, it puckers the meat, crinkling the sausage's skin.

"What the fuck?"

It is not a nice *what the fuck*. He does not kid. I've seen his kitchen rage, sharp-toothed and profound, but I've never felt it directed at me.

"I'm sorry, Ari," I say, appealing to his compassion. I work beside him all day and night because I care about him, care about this restaurant, his passion, maybe ours. My head is spinny, my mouth dry, feet sore, forearm singed. "I messed up. I'm trying."

His eyes are shrivelly, suddenly, like the raisins he makes from Concord grapes. "Trying? I showed you how to do this."

He had indeed demonstrated, patiently. The perfect slice was made using the pointy end of the knife, with lots of confidence and speed, pulling laterally, rather than up and down. I had listened and watched, but not exactly mastered the technique. But this, I had to admit, was a particularly ugly cut.

"It's not that bad," I say, hurt.

He doesn't argue. Ari picks up the plate in his big hands, cocks it back, his sinewy bicep swinging toward the ceiling, chucks it past my shoulder, past James's head. It flies fast through the air, shatters into many pieces and plate-dust in the open garden door. The sausage tumbles into a flower bed.

I think, *My boyfriend just threw a plate at me.*

I follow the plate into the garden, stand against a tree, its trunk holding me so I won't fall to the ground. My face is wet with tears and sweat and anger. Ari doesn't come after me. He has to finish table 7, table 12.

I can hear chatter from the dining room, the crescendo of jazz from the speakers, the whir of the dishwasher. My eyes burn. The garden is in bloom, stupendous, enclosed with brick walls, some green with climbing ivy. I want to climb with it, into the sweet night, away from this place, but I take off my bandana, wipe my face, head back into the kitchen's bellow.

That night I realize I want out.

We've been running the restaurant together for more than a year. We've put on five weddings and seventeen private dinners and hundreds of nights of service. We've added brunch and live jazz in the bar on Tuesdays. We've installed a POS system, repainted, hung new art. We've gotten out of bed and run to the restaurant at 4 AM because the walk-in fizzled in the heat of summer and loaded sides of beef into ice-filled coolers. The menu changes nearly every night.

Our vision. Our dream. The truth is, I don't love it or even like it. I am simultaneously stressed and bored. I don't want to have my own restaurant anymore or work in someone else's. I love food as much as ever, more, gooseberries sweet as sunrise, the ooze of a snowy burrata, the buzz of a good service, the dance, but I am tired of twelve-hour shifts and counting the cash at obscene hours. I'm tired of every night feeling somehow the same. The bottoms of my feet always throb, my lower back torments me. By the end of the night, I have used up so much niceness, all my niceness for my staff, my regulars, Ari, special events, bridal showers, I'm certain I won't have any left. I'm afraid to look in the mirror. I'm surely a monster. I'm twenty-three.

I still think Ari is gorgeous, a genius, but my heart has contracted. Loving him is a memory. I need a change. I want out of restaurantland. I can't work with Ari anymore.

I think he will be relieved when I tell him I want to break up. We barely talk, except to go over the menu for the night, an invoice for heirloom beans, a writer at table 7. I walk Nuni after work alone. We sleep as far away from each other on the mattress as we can without rolling onto the floor. He threw a plate at me.

Ari is not relieved. He cries and cries and pleads and tells me I'm right, that things must change. He will quit smoking. He will let his cooks clean after service without him so that we can go home together. He will cook for us again.

But it is too late. My heart is not in it.

"Hannah Chamuda," he says. "You are terribly selfish."

I wonder if I am terribly selfish. I probably am. I cry, too. I thought this was what I wanted: the restaurant, the boyfriend. But having them, I can't wait to be free from them.

I think of what else I could do. I have nearly seven years in restaurantland under my belt, and I don't want an eighth. I've always loved to write. Before I walk the four blocks from my apartment to Elle Restaurant, every day but Monday, I freelance. A story here, a story there, a series on food entrepreneurs for a finance website.

One of my profiles is on Steve Jenkins, the godfather of Fairway. He runs the cheese department there, the olive oil program. He's a big deal. He wrote *The Cheese Primer*, which I have stashed behind the cheese display at Elle. I have long passages on triple crèmes and cheddars memorized. Talking to Steve is great fun. I leave my interview inspired.

After the plate-throwing incident, I send Steve an email: "I loved talking with you and admire what you do. Are you hiring at Fairway?"

After many hours of bus rides from Philly to NYC and back again, interviews with long lineups of executives, buyers, waiting by the shopping carts, sharing a still-warm ball of mozzarella with Steve, it looks like I have the job.

We're sitting at a Burger King on 86th Street next to the new Upper East Side Fairway, slated to open any minute, drinking inky coffee. "Congratulations." It's Bill, Fairway's CEO, who shakes my hand. "We really like you but we're not quite sure what to do with you. Why don't you start behind the cheese counter while we figure it out?"

Behind the cheese counter is a great place to start. Restaurant people wear clogs; grocery people wear sneakers. Each morning, I lace up my new sneakers and walk across Central Park to the brand new Upper East Side Fairway. It's blinding, shiny with newness. I buy a cinnamon tea at the discounted employee rate and stash it beside the disposable gloves, rolls of paper towels. I get up close and very personal with the ashy Morbier, Gouda dotted with crunchy crystals, the oozy stink of Langres. I stretch the curds into mozzarella myself, pulling until my forearms are sore and my thoughts are milky and happy. I help women plan dinner parties: *Your guests will love Midnight Moon; if I'm wrong come back and I'll buy you a leg of lamb.* I am patient with old men and their long instructions for the perfect piece of farmer's cheese. I learn to break down a wheel of Parmigiano-Reggiano into perfect wedges, wrap them tight as my leggings.

Ari thinks this job is a stupid idea. "What, you're going to put boxes of things on shelves?" Ari cooked at Per Se, *staged* at Bouley. He cares about Michelin stars, soigné slips, Japanese turnips transformed to silk. Grocery stores do not register.

He keeps the apartment in Philadelphia. Ari keeps Nuni, too. I want the puppy but I feel guilty; it was my choice to break up. I miss Nuni. I surprise myself, missing Ari.

Six weeks later, Bill stops by the cheese counter. "We have a job for you. Come to the office tomorrow morning."

"That's amazing! What is it?"

"You'll find out all about it then."

I wake up early to wash my hair and dry it. I put on my motorcycle boots instead of my now-scuffed sneakers and ride the 1 train up to 125th Street. When I arrive at Steve's office, I think I have arrived in heaven. It is the least glamorous place. It has the aesthetics of a low security prison or a muffler shop. There are bars on the windows and puffs of stuffing breaking loose from old leather chairs.

And yet! Every surface is covered in bottles of olive oil and vinegar, tins of Alsatian sauerkraut, *pruneaux d'Agen,* Bixi Bixia (the great Basque barbecue sauce made with Espelette pepper), little jars of garum, the unfathomably stinky Roman fish sauce Steve's friend has been making from Spanish mackerel. Tins of popcorn and butter cookies and licorice candies are stacked nearly to the ceiling.

I never learn what my job is; I just do whatever Steve needs. I take over the Fairway blog. I write signs for new products like Banyuls vinegar and Sicilian pesto, red with plum tomato. When a reporter calls to ask about green almonds or soft shells, they pass the phone to me. Whatever it is, I like it. It suits me.

Steve tilts his head back and takes a big swig straight from a bottle of olive oil. "Taste this," he says, a few times a day, passing the bottle. Always I am glad when I do.

When Steve has a few moments, he taps me on the shoulder, gathers us around the conference table, unfolds a ratty map, and begins a geography lesson.

Fairway is in full expansion mode. Some mornings, Steve picks me up in the Rocket Ship, his beautiful, expensive Audi. We ride to the new suburban Fairways: Little Falls, New Jersey, or Douglaston, Queens, and he plays really good music, really loud, and gives me reading assignments. Thanks to Steve, I discover Waverley Root, Roy Andries de Groot, and Patience Gray. I read *When French Women Cook* by Madeleine Kamman in two sittings.

"Didn't the chapter on Provence make you cry?"

"Absolutely."

Back at home, my mom texts and asks if I want to have dinner with her friends on the Upper East Side. I say "Sure." I put on my moto boots and walk across Central Park. I'm thinking of the lavender in Provence in *When French Women Cook*, the way it turns whole fields purple, how different it must smell than it does right here in New York autumn, crisp, the leaves lit up as if burning on their trees. It's the night of my last binge.

Olive Oil

"Hi," I say at my first recovery meeting, because I have nothing to lose. "I'm Hannah. I think I'm a compulsive eater. I'm pretty sure, actually."

My stomach is still queasy from my binge. We're near Union Square, in a stark room in a community center atop a bodega. Everyone holds hands and says a prayer I don't know. My palms are slick with fear. The last sun of the day burns between vertical shades drawn shut.

A short, trim man with a crisp suit talks first. He passes around pictures: same tremendous smile on a different body. He must have lost a hundred pounds, more. The words that come out of his mouth are unlike any I have heard.

"I ate to fill the God-sized hole in my soul. I kept eating and eating and it was never enough."

"Compulsive eating is a disease. Like alcoholism. Like cancer. We don't have this thing because we're weak-willed or morally corrupt. We have it because we have it. We have it because we are compulsive overeaters."

"I found a way out. There is an answer here. Today, I am free."

I have so many questions. I adjust my skirt to cover the cold metal of the folding chair. The people around me are old and young, fat and thin. There are no scales or lists of foods to eat and not eat.

After the speaker finishes, we go around and share. I think, *Why not?* "Hi, this is my first meeting. I can't remember a time when I didn't want to eat until it hurt. I feel like I belong here. I had no idea something like this existed. I'm so happy it does."

People talk about the things I have done, things I have never spoken out loud. Hiding food, stealing food, lying, throwing away food then digging into the trash can to retrieve it, puking, trying to puke, a million hours at the gym, elaborate mind games, starving, bingeing, raging, obsession, obsession . . .

And then something miraculous happens: lightning does not strike them dead. They do not faint from embarrassment. They do not hang their heads low in shame. They smile, nod knowingly. Their nods say "I get it." They laugh and laugh. They get up from their plastic folding chairs and hold hands again. Then they give each other big hugs, put on their coats, and walk out into the night.

I buy myself a diet cream soda at the bodega. I feel full of bubbles in the best way. I can't believe such a place exists. I can't wait to go back.

Home after that first meeting, Ari calls. His voice sounds like honey, like the jar of New Zealand Manuka he kept on our counter, floral and crystalline. His Israeli accent is still as thick as it, too, although he's lived here for ten years, eleven now. He says, "I can't believe you brought me to this horrible city and then left me here."

I didn't bring him to Philly. It was his idea to pack up his place in Forest Hills and move into the apartment I had just myself unpacked. I was brand new to the city, too. I know he hates it there, in the city of brotherly love.

"I'm sorry," I say a million times, because it hurts me to hurt him. I wish things were different. But my mind is made up. It's over between us.

Still, I miss the way he'd roll up his jeans and bleach our bathroom when he was stressed, the wholeheartedness of his scrubbing.

Sometimes he'd wash my hair in the shower, twirling a bubbly pile atop my head. I would make him coffee with exactly one and a half spoonfuls of sugar. Everything he did was methodical, unequivocal, and he expected the same of me. In my new apartment, I don't make the bed, a small rebellion. I miss his joy at summer's first tomatoes, fall's sweet pears, his long arms around me at night. *Laila tov*, he would say, which means good night in Hebrew. I'd listen to his chest fill up with air, his exhale hot as steam on my neck.

But I also remember his rage and his ruthlessness, his quiet cruelty at home. I sleep submerged in the bed that is all mine. I do not dream of Ari.

The next day I head to another support group meeting after work. It is in the West Village, the streets deserting their neat grids for crisscrossed chaos. I'm not sure where I'm going. I walk around in a circle, another. The sky opens up into sheets of austere rain. Umbrellaless, water drips off my hair, my eyelashes. I think about turning around and riding the subway back home to 95th Street.

Then there it is, a community center with walls the color of Listerine. My wet shoes squeak across the shiny floor. The room is packed. I slide into a seat in the back. Someone smiles at me. In the front, a woman my mother's age is talking. She crosses her long legs, which wear high boots with high heels. Her laughter chimes like bells.

She tells her story—what it was like, what happened, and what it's like now. I learn later that this is the formula for a pitch. A pitch, like a sales pitch. "This is my story . . ." There are no leaders, no stars or VIPs, they say. Just a lot of bozos on the bus. Bozos with stories.

Her name is Faith. *I used to throw fancy dinner parties,* she says, *then eat every scrap of everything leftover, standing up, the moment the last guest shut the door behind me. If there was a cake, I was in serious trouble. I would throw away the cake, pour coffee grounds on top to try to stop myself from eating it. But it was no use. I'd dig it out, wipe off the coffee grounds, devour it.* She told us about being a fat kid, summers at fat camp, gaining everything back and more, showing up at fat camp fatter than ever one summer and then another. The grapefruit diet, the cabbage soup diet, the Diet Coke and cigarettes diet. A silent retreat, a sweat lodge. A go at intuitive eating. *If the diets worked, I wouldn't be here.* The room is rapt. Her story is my story.

The woman sitting next to me is pregnant, enormously so, and she rests her hands on her belly. There are thin girls and fat girls, a man in a bow tie, cat's eye glasses, sneakers and pointy heels, backpacks and designer bags and totes. Models, graduate students, retirees, talk show hosts, personal chefs, investment bankers. The star of the latest everyone-is-staying-up-all-night-to-watch Netflix series is bawling her eyes out. Someone hands her a tissue, slings an arm around her shoulder. She is famous, and it makes me feel better, that nobody is immune from this pain. That we have a place to go. I can't believe she is here, or that I am here.

We have everything and nothing in common. *This is the last house on the block*, they say. We have tried every diet, every scheme. We are out of ideas, and so we come here.

People share: *I just want to know how to make it through a night.*

I can't count how many times I have polished off my roommate's food.

I thought I was too fat to celebrate my birthday. But this year, I celebrated my birthday anyway. Thanks to recovery.

I went to a hotel and the towel wouldn't wrap all the way around my body.

I got rid of the clothes that were too big.

I got rid of the clothes that were too small.

I feel the sweet unfurling of relief. We are in this ugly room because of pain, not strength. And yet I feel stronger than I have in a long time, as if I'm swimming in a dense sea of power and love. These are my people. I raise my hand to share, but this time the room is packed and nobody calls on me. I'm happy just to listen. After the meeting, I go to talk to Faith. She has a crowd around her, so I wait my turn.

"Thank you," I say. "I'm new. This is my second meeting. Every word you said rang true for me. I've never heard anyone talk like that, say this stuff out loud."

"Here," she says, her smile like sustenance, pulling a pen out of her purse and scribbling something in a book. She presses the book into my hands. "Call me!"

On the way home, I open the blue cover. *Alcoholics Anonymous Big Book Pocket Edition*, it says in serious-looking print. In Faith's swirly cursive: *Buckle your seat belt, it's going to be a wild ride! Love, Faith.* Underneath there is her phone number. I put the book by my bed, wake up with it open on my chest.

When I meet Nick, I am sitting at my desk, writing a blog post about our new Lambrusco vinegar, which everyone is in a tizzy about. It is beautiful vinegar—pink, fizzy. We pass around the bottle, admiring our new baby. Steve takes a swig, straight from the bottle's cool glass mouth. The rest of us drizzle from its nozzle over our arugula salads at lunchtime.

Nick comes by and everyone erupts—"Nutty Nick! Nickster!"— and gives him hugs. Steve introduces us and Nick shakes my hand with his big hand. The air around him is different. Nick is tall and blond. All American. Ocean eyes. My heartbeat is a drum.

I don't see Nick for another month. I hear talk around the office about Nick, and I listen. Nick is the son of the once-beloved owner who sold out to the private equity guys. There are rumors that Nick's dad made the new owners promise to make sure his son had a job, now and always. He grew up in the aisles of the market, playing hide-and-seek behind the deli counter. There is a sandwich named after him. They say Nick was a fuckup—drugs, drinking, general fucking up—but he is redeemed. The prodigal Fairway son. I wonder what it would be like to work at the opus your dad created. I wonder if Nick is like Corey.

Steve says I should spend more time in the stores, that Nick can show me around the flagship on 74th Street. We make a plan for 3 PM, but Nick isn't there. I buy a giant apple and walk up Broadway all the way home, crunching on its flesh.

I'm sorry! Nick emails. *My back was a mess and I had to go to the chiropractor and it was the only appointment. Tomorrow?*

But tomorrow I have a day full of meetings, and the company decides Nick will leave his post as the 74th Street store manager and instead travel around to all the stores, ten stores now, and more all the time, and make sure Steve's products—we call them Steve's products, the golden olive oils from Tuscany and Provence, the tins of Brittany vintage sardines, *sel gris* from Guérande, Moroccan preserved lemons—get properly ordered and merchandized and understood. That the signs I write get printed out and laminated and hung on little rings we buy from Staples.

Nick comes back to the office, more hugs. This time I get a hug. He unpacks the contents of his backpack onto my desk: signs for garlic artichoke dip and *olio santo* (the "sacred oil," the very best from the harvest), staplers, a price gun that looks like a kid's toy gun.

"Help Nick out," Steve says. "The best way to get to know the products intimately is to get your hands on 'em." I know this to be true.

It's always cold in the store, hundreds of refrigerators pumping chill. Up in the office, I grab a fleece from a big cardboard box that says "Hands Off!!"

Nick and I go to work reorganizing the oil section. We pull everything off the shelves, hundreds of bottles and tins, thousands. We load up a shopping cart and then another. I touch sesame and grapeseed and avocado, but the ones we fuss over, the ones that make us famous, are our extra-virgin beauties. We try to memorize the bottles, but there are more than a hundred. They come from Extremadura, Andalucía,

Provence, western Sicilia, Sardegna, Liguria, Peloponnese, Baja Mexico, Ribatejo in the north of Portugal, California. Once in a while we pause our work to open a bottle and pour its insides into little plastic cups from the deli to taste. The best olives light a match in the back of my throat.

"This one is great," Nick says, holding up an Argentinian stunner. "Let's make a whole display of it." And again, we replot the course of our work.

Nick has a vision. A million visions. We're going to hang up a world map, arrange the bottles on the shelves geographically. The globe imagined in olive oil.

The next morning, I ask Steve if I can keep working with Nick. "Knock your socks off," he tells me. I wear sneakers so I can spend all day on the squeaky linoleum floors, two sweaters. Still, my fingers turn so cold I hold them under my armpits and wiggle. The fluorescent lights paint everything brassy. Shoppers stop to hug Nick, ask him about his dad, about rye bread.

While working, we talk. Nick's words fly, and I feel wildly awake. He makes me laugh so hard I have to hold on to the shelves, put down the oils so they don't shatter and spray the store with shards of glass and grease. This menial labor feels like the sweetest adventure.

Nick tells me about his best friend's band, how they were almost famous in the nineties, but their record label screwed them over. Sometimes he sings with the band still, plays the hell out of his guitar. He tells me about how he used to work for SNL, wonders how his life would have unfolded if he stayed with TV instead of leaving to work for his dad. "I wanted to be close to my dad, but he didn't want to be close to me."

"It's never too late," I say.

We spray the bottles with Windex, wipe them lustrous. We laugh until my belly cramps.

Is he flirting? He's flirting. He's forty-one, I have just turned twenty-four. What is it with these older men? I feel older than all of them.

Nick rolls up his T-shirt and flexes his biceps. Girls and moms stop by while he's stocking shelves to chat, lob a question about balsamic. They blush. The whole world knows he's ridiculously cute. Better, magnetic. Energy pools at his feet. When he speaks, people listen.

The air is humming with energy, firefighters in full gear plucking things off shelves for lunch. A chef in his white coat pushes a whole side of some kind of animal, wrapped like a present with brown paper and twine. It fills a whole shopping cart.

Ari stops calling and I stop missing him. But when he emails, *Hannah, can we talk, it's important,* I dial him right away.

"Don't worry," he tells me. His voice sounds punctured, the honey is gone. "I'm not trying to get you back anymore. It's for the best. I'm sorry I blamed my unhappiness on you."

"Oh, it's okay, really. We both did our best." I mean it. I realize I have forgiven him, feel almost light with forgiveness.

"There's something I have to tell you. It's important to me that you know. It's been a really hard time for me. I was in the hospital for a few weeks. I'm recovering."

"Oh my god, Ari. Oh my god." And again, "I'm so sorry. Are you okay?"

"Stop being sorry. I'm so much better now. You don't need to worry. I'm leaving Elle Restaurant. It is silly being there without you. Maybe I'll go back to Jerusalem. Maybe I'll go back to New York. Don't worry, not for you. Things look different now. I don't want you to do anything. I don't want you to feel sorry for me. I just wanted you to know."

When we hang up, I open up the little book and call Faith. She answers and I tell her about Ari through snaggy tears.

"Oh honey," she says. "We are powerless over more than just food. We are powerless over other people."

"I can't believe I wasn't there for him."

"It wasn't your job to be. He was your ex-boyfriend, not your boyfriend."

I didn't ask him what happened. At night, I dream of the worst: that he needed me and I left him behind. I wonder if he is telling me the truth, then feel guilty for wondering.

"What should I do?" I want someone to tell me.

"Take care of yourself. Pray for him. Don't hurt yourself with food." It sounds so simple, but I cannot think of sitting with disquiet that circles me like wolves. I think about how many bars of chocolate it may take for my head to go silent, cones of ice cream. "Your feelings won't kill you," Faith says as if reading my mind. "And they will pass. Promise."

I go for a walk, down to the Fairway at 74th Street. It cheers me up, as it always does, mountains of gleaming grapes, sides of dry-aged beef, golden olive oils in lovely bottles packed ceiling high, lines of shoppers waiting for James the smoked salmon maestro to slice their lox into translucent ribbons, dole out pickled herring. Even the mean old ladies, bulldozing me with their shopping carts, elbows poised as weapons, make me happy. I say hi to Ken, my favorite manager. He won't let me pay for my seltzer.

It feels a small miracle: that night I neither binge my brains out nor starve myself. My two security blankets. Without them I am alone with my sadness, bitter as the spiciest olive oil, more vinegary than pickled herring.

"If I wasn't married, I'd ask you out in a heartbeat," Nick tells me. My torso is wedged in a shelf; I'm pulling out some dusty blends of unfiltered olive oil from Lazio. I unfurl myself from the shelf, the air suddenly shockingly cold on my neck.

"I didn't know you were married," I say. "I've been harboring a little crush on you."

He doesn't wear a ring. I'm taken aback double: that he's married and that he likes me. We both laugh a little.

"Can we still grab lunch?" he asks.

"Of course."

Monday it is falafel; Tuesday, pizza. Wednesday we go to the local hardware store together to pick up hooks to hang the signs I wrote about Sicilian pesto. We weave past paintbrushes and casserole pans. By the flashlights and screwdrivers he stops, and so I stop, too. I notice he is not breathing, and I am not breathing, and everything is still. His hand on my face. A kiss so soft I couldn't be sure it is happening, if not for my skin and belly hot as fever, my heart a live wire.

It's not a long kiss, but we stand there after, quiet, shocked, changed. Nick buys the hooks. Out in Harlem, the traffic and sunlight are cacophony.

On the way back to work, we duck behind a bus stop. We stand there with our faces almost touching. Bus, no bus, I don't know. We kiss again. The kiss opens up at my feet, and I fall into the sea of it. We can't stop kissing.

We kiss everywhere. He brings bags of groceries to my apartment, whistles while he unpacks them into my cabinets. We cook chicken thighs together in our new Burgundian mustard on the grill pan in my studio, filling up the apartment with mustardy smoke. We take our dinner upstairs to the roof of my apartment building. I sit between his knees, watch the sun disappear behind brick and skyline, his chest strong and urgent against my back.

"These are really good chicken thighs," I say, and he kisses me. We float.

When we're together the barometric pressure drops. The weight of the air in the atmosphere undulates, I feel it surge and swell. He says he feels it, too. It's unimaginable.

He is the best drug, and I am an instant fiend.

We browse bookstores and read each other poems, recipes, dance ridiculously and beautifully, walk through Central Park, our fingertips looped around each other's.

"Let's play a game." And we hopscotch down Riverside. He picks me up, and I ride like an elated child on his back, my legs squeezing his hips, my arms around his neck. He drops me in the grass of the Great Lawn, tickles me 'til it hurts.

"Hannus Maximus, I've lived here all my life, but this whole city is new with you."

"I have to tell you something." I have made up my mind to tell Nick about my eating disorder, about recovery. "I used to have a really bad eating disorder. I still do, sort of. It's so much better, though. I'm in recovery."

"Oh! I'm in recovery, too. Or I should be. I go to meetings sometimes, but I should go much more."

"For what? Is it okay that I ask?"

"The standard. Booze. Cocaine."

I don't think, *Hannah, yikes, walk away.* I think, *Thank god. I am not alone. He gets it.*

I go with Nick to set up the new stores in Woodland Park, Kips Bay, Nanuet. He picks me up from my apartment, drives the Zipcar, I navigate up the West Side Highway or down the Garden State. We sing along to the playlists he has made for the occasion. We hang up signs and he puts up shelves, his body vibrating with the buzz of the electric drill. We make a display of soft-dried French figs, stacking them tall, and sneak out for omelets at local diners. He plays Pearl Jam on the jukebox. We kiss until my lips go tingly and numb.

When I'm with him, my brain quiets a little, but when he goes home to Elena, the guilt is unbearable. I worry. I know it was Nick, not I, who stood in a church thirteen years ago and vowed 'til death do them part, then asked me to lunch, kissed me in the hardware store, whispers to me it's me and not her he loves, needs me like food and oxygen. But I share the responsibility. I kiss him back. I wait for his texts. The longing to be as close to him as possible grips me until I am savage with it.

From the beginning, I cannot do this, and I cannot not do this.

It fucks with my own perception of myself. I never thought of myself as the mistress type, which feels an old-fashioned term. I have friends in open relationships, but this is not that.

"Maybe Elena would understand?" I ask. I know it is far-fetched.

"It would destroy her."

I tell only Urs.

"Oh honey," she says. "This does not sound good. You deserve better."

I deserve better. So does Nick. So does Elena.

One night, Steve invites us to a party at a swanky midtown loft. It has something to do with the Canadian embassy. There will be fancy maple syrup, butter tarts, a new Canadian whiskey. I put on a blue dress, eyeliner. Steve drives me in the Rocket Ship.

There are men in suits and women in stilettos, little black dresses, clinking glasses of champagne. Through the window, Manhattan gleams. Nick is there already, and I beeline to the space filled with him.

"Hi," I say, touch his arm. I feel pretty, today, because of my just-a-bit-shimmery blue dress and maybe because Nick thinks I'm pretty, tells me so, looks at me with full eyes.

"Hi. You look nice." But his eyes don't say so. Tonight, they look despondent.

"Are you okay?"

"This whole thing is a lot of bullshit," he says.

"Sure. But it's fun regardless. I like to watch the bullshit."

Nick turns away, and so I go talk to Steve, our other coworkers. Steve introduces me to the pinstripe-suited guy from the Canadian embassy. I ask him questions about Canada, and he launches into a story about wintertime, the waves crashing against Nova Scotia. I eat a maple sugar candy. The sugar dissolves into my mouth, my bloodstream.

"Let's get out of here, let's get some dinner." Steve and the crew invite me, invite Nick.

"I can't go," Nick says, averting his eyes.

"Come with us!" It feels incredibly important that he be there with me in my blue dress. But he turns around and walks up 6th Avenue, his blond head disappearing into the crowd.

He texts minutes later: *I can't believe you went without me.*

Why didn't you join us? I wanted you to be here. You can still come! Please come. There's space! We pile into a bar, our puffy coats stacked on stools. I am self-conscious, texting Nick when I should be chatting with my still-new coworkers, but my head pounds with whiskey and sugar, and Nick matters more than anything right now. I think about leaving to find him.

I can't be there.

Why? We all want you here. I really want you here.

His words fill my screen. *Hannah, I can't take it. Everyone is checking you out. You are flirting with the Canadian dude and I can't do anything about it. You are not mine.*

You are not mine.

He has a wife. A wife of thirteen years. He is going home to his wife. I think of them sitting together on their plush couch, his arm around her, him asking about her day, them having sex, because that's what people do when they're married. I wonder if she suspects her husband is in love with a girl from work. I bury my phone deep in the bottom of my purse.

"What are you drinking?" Steve asks, and orders me a frothy beer, sweet and cold as a milkshake.

"Nick's like a son, but he's trouble. He's no good for you. Don't get mixed up with him, Hanner." Everyone seems to have a different nick-name for me. I nod and drink my beer and listen to gossip about the arugula guy who is involved in the Mafia, the butcher's coke problem. Steve drives me home in the Rocket Ship. Inside I unzip my blue dress, curl up, eyeliner still on. My bed is vast around me; it may swallow me whole in its great mattress belly.

The next morning, clarity wells up in my throat, caustic. In the shower's pummel, I know what I have not wanted to tell myself: this cannot end well. I have never cheated and here I am, the other woman. I have to end this before the wormhole of this love spits me somewhere soundless and dire. I feel woozy, unwieldy from last night's drinks, but the truth steadies me.

I pick up my phone, text: *You're right. This is not fair to anyone. I can't do this anymore.*

But the buzzer rings in my apartment and Nick is downstairs. I am not expecting him. In the mirror, my face looks overcast. I put on a tank top.

He comes up with oatmeal, blueberries, two coffees.

"I'm so sorry," he says. "I brought breakfast."

"Nick, you can't just show up randomly. I am not your girlfriend." Outside, the hum of morning rush hour traffic, its horns and low shouts.

"What, do you have a guy over?"

"Of course not."

"What do you mean I can't show up? I love you."

"I love you, too."

He says I love you first, and then it is a mantra: *I love you. I love you. I love you.*

He kicks off his sneakers, sits on my sofa. The enormity of his presence makes my apartment feel miniature. "Hannah," he says, "I'm forty-one years old. I've lived, what, seventeen years more than you. This does not happen every day. I've never felt the weight of the atmosphere drop with anyone in forty-one years."

"I've never felt it, either."

"We can't just throw it away like nothing happened. This feeling. People die for it."

"I know. I know. But it's not right. What about your wife?" I hate saying her name. It feels like sand in my throat. Elena.

Nick is careful never to utter a negative word about Elena. Having cheated on her with me and everything that entails—lies tiny and immense, a million betrayals—it seems a small gesture, but still somehow an important one. I dream about her pouring pickle juice over my head until my lips are caked in brine. I dream that she tears the nails off my fingers and toes, one at a time, with relish. It doesn't hurt. It feels good.

I don't know Elena, but I feel a sort of intimacy with her. We both love Nick. There are things I know about her, like that she is a real estate attorney, she drives a big car, she does the laundry and folds it into impossibly neat parcels, she is meticulous about using hand sanitizer. I collect these details like treasures.

"Give me time. It's complicated. Thirteen years is a long time. Her family is like family to me. We have a home together. She took care of me when I was at my worst. She never gave up on me."

"Okay, fine. So go to her now, then."

"I can't. I know you understand. The atmosphere stays the same with her. I've never felt the way I feel with you with her or with anyone. We're going to go our separate ways. It's just going to take some time."

We have this conversation hundreds, thousands of times, about us. About falling in love with someone else and being married. About the right thing to do, and the possible thing. *I can't do it,* I say again and again. *Work out your life and call me when you're not married to another woman. I love you. We deserve better, we deserve the real deal, we deserve to do it right.*

But then, after an hour or a day or maybe a week of silence, we talk again. He is waiting for me at my desk at work. He brings a new olive oil to try, fancy headphones, a drawing he made of us together: Nefarious Nick and Hannus Maximus, wide smiles in blue ink, him with his guitar and me with my pen, wielded like a dart in my stick-figure hand. ("You'll write our story one day," he tells me.) We walk down Riverside Park, the leaves crunching at our feet. We talk until our words grow wings and fly off over the Hudson. He makes me understand that he understands. He makes me laugh. Back in my apartment, in the cavernous space of his chest, the world stops spinning all together. I know it's the wrong thing to do, to love him, but I also know I have no choice.

Later, I wonder if I could have stopped it before it began. Maybe before the pizza lunch, or the hardware store kiss. Definitely before having him over to 95th Street, his damn guitar, the songs, the sex. But I don't think I could have stopped it at all. My head said *no, no, no, no, no fucking way.* But my heart said *yes. Yes and yes and yes.*

Nick leaves one of his guitars at my apartment, stops by after work to sing songs he writes for me. There's a new song every day. I record them on my phone. Sometimes I write them lyrics, scribbling lines as he thrums and strums and wails. When he is out of songs, we turn on

Cake and sing along, dance and jump like crazy people until collapsing in laughter.

My doormen know Nick—he brings them bagels from the shop next door, coffee with all the fixings when he visits, which soon becomes every day. Usually he comes before work. Elena works super early, so Nick doesn't need an elaborate story. I'm still in bed when the buzzer buzzes, foggy. We kiss and I make us Irish oats on my stove. We share a cab together, holding hands across the slick leather seats. He takes a walk around the block before heading in, just in case. We don't want our coworkers to see us arriving together.

After work, we drink quartinos of red wine at the wine bar around the corner, my leg slung over his leg on the tall barstools. Nick wants to sit way back in the corner, just in case, as everyone seems to know him, the Fairway guy, the mayor of the Upper West Side.

I've never watched anyone drink the way Nick drinks. It frightens me. He starts out slow, like anyone starts, a sip, Malbec darkening the creases of his soft lips. He speeds up and up, one, two, three quartinos slide down his throat, then we're off to the store to buy a few bottles, which are empty before I finish the glass I pour myself. I understand. He drinks the way I eat—to fill something unfillable.

Somewhere midbottle he is texting the coke dealer, making plans to meet him outside Two Boots pizzeria, which I'm okay with because I love the pie with soppressata, the sweet ooze of mozzarella, the corn-meal-dusted crust, which I chew on while we wait, his knee bouncing out the seconds 'til the guy arrives with his little baggies of white stuff, slides them into Nick's palm.

His words speed up, suddenly shrill, he makes jokes with no punch lines, then tells the same jokes again. His joy turns fast into a sort of brutal anger, and everything around him is suddenly all wrong, perverse, an enemy. I'm glad he's going to go—home, or out to his next stop of the night. Suddenly I can't wait to be rid of him. Watching Nick transform into another person is unnerving. Nutty Nick, they call him. Or Naughty Nicky.

I panic. Who is this guy, and why am I here? I am embarrassed for him, but mostly for myself. "Shit," he says. "I have like twelve missed calls from Elena." My stomach tastes like motor oil.

"You should go."

I'm tired and ready to be horizontal, to be far away from this man who I may or may not know.

When I'm not at work or with Nick, I'm at meetings. They feel like home. I hear people talk about what I used to do, still do: look at every single box of cereal at the grocery store to see which has the fewest calories, try to "save up" those calories for a binge I know is coming. They know what it is like to look at yourself in the mirror and feel punched.

Men have this thing, too. In recovery, I meet a hipster man in his twenties: gingham, tight pants. He says that for seven years, all he consumed in daylight was two liters of Diet Coke and iced coffee, black. Then at night he came home, arms heavy with grocery bags. He drew the shades and binged his brains out on Entenmann's cookies and pepperoni pizza and vanilla ice cream, then puked until he fell asleep to the lingering smell of his own vomit, a sea of empty Entenmann's boxes, pizza. He looks normal. His eyes shine like tinsel.

Joel, the artist, looks normal, too. He's fiftyish, he has a little girl who wakes him up at ungodly hours for tea parties with the whole gang of household dolls. Nine times out of ten, he complies. Joel is sort of a B-list celebrity, a Buddhist, a mayor of the East Village. Joel reads my poems and has something to say, even about the worst ones. His voice is like taffeta. He shows me pictures of when he was four hundred pounds, more, two Joels, and then when he was anorexic, half a Joel, his chin and ears pointy on a face that has nothing to do with the face that smiles at me now.

Ben is a modern Orthodox Jew. He's distinguished, a successful doctor, fancy suits, family, dogs, multiple households. He wears a yarmulke on his balding head. He says being a compulsive eater is more agonizing that the leukemia he battles. "Nothing brings me to my knees like sugar," he says. He tells about sneaking out of the hospital, his wife in labor, to get his sugar fix. "The physical pain is hard. The way I hurt myself, now that's suffering." The things we do to ourselves, the disease does to us.

This is not just a problem for teenage girls. We are young and old, rich and poor, all the colors, gay, straight, transgender. We are everyone. We have this thing and it is killing us.

But mostly there are girls and women. I meet Jenny, a singer with one Grammy under her belt, maybe two. Jenny also runs a nonprofit. Her blonde hair is soft down her back. She turns heads. She's celebrating two years out of inpatient rehab for anorexia, and we're drinking sparkling rosé by a fireplace in a Brooklyn bar to celebrate the occasion. How does a woman, any woman, possibly escape from this thing?

The fire lights her up. "They want you skinny. Our culture adores skinny. When I lost weight, all I heard was praise and more praise. I'd arrived. Finally I was valued. People looked at me differently, paid more attention. Compliments poured like rain. It didn't matter how I did it, how miserable I was, how deeply fucked.

"And then, suddenly," she says, leaning forward, her fingernails long around her wine glass, "I've gone too far, broken some kind of tenuous, invisible boundary and people's kudos turn to concern. I've gone from the object of envy to that of scorn, pity because I'm doing exactly the same thing. Not because I've started dieting but because I cannot stop. One hundred twenty pounds, and I'm a hero. One hundred and five, and I'm a pariah.

"We're supposed to be just-enough screwed up," she says that night. "And that's acceptable, even necessary. And then, when the screwed up takes over, everyone wonders what happened."

"I know," I tell her. "The same thing happened to me."

It helps every time, this new knowledge that I am not alone with this.

"Elena is going away this weekend," Nick tells me one day at my place. The sun is drifting up out of my window. He's stroking his guitar on his lap like a pet. "I'm going to stay over."

"Aren't you going to ask me?"

He looks slapped. "Hannah, I would be deeply honored to stay here this weekend with you."

The night before, I toss and turn but don't sleep.

We spend twenty-four hours in bed. I can't bear the thought of him staying. I can't bear the thought of him going.

Winter thaws, and I decide to have my family over for Mother's Day, now that I have my own apartment. I tell Nick. I tell him I hate that he is a secret.

"I know," he says. "Let me at least help you out."

It is my first time hosting family, which feels significant, grown-up. I am roasting chicken and making a veggie risotto. I pick out what music I'll play, what wine I'll serve in what glasses.

"I wish you could be here," I tell him. I wish it bad.

"Me too," he says. "Soon." He has his pleading eyes. He cleans the top of the fridge. He Swiffers under the bed. He shakes the rugs out the window. "I have to go," he says. He kisses me goodbye, a quick kiss.

I open the windows and turn up the music. There is only a little cleaning left. I begin scrubbing my kitchen tiles with a bleachy rag. Then a wet spot under my bare foot fells me and I am on the floor, my arm jutting at a funky angle beneath me.

It hurts, bad. It is late and I am tired; I pop ibuprofen, turn on the TV, and hope I will nod off and wake up bruised but fine. But I can feel my pulse in my forearm, and a surge of heat in my face, and pain like a much-too-tight jacket.

I miss Nick, his just-shaven face soft against my own, or singing sweet in the shower.

I call my dad. My dad is good in emergencies big and tiny. "Ice," he says. "Elevation. Call the nurse hotline—there's a number on the insurance card. I love you."

When I tell the Southern-accented lady over the phone that I can't bend my arm, that the pain is coming in jarring crests, she suggests the ER. "Saturday night in New York," she says kindly. "Bring a book."

It is a few minutes after eleven, the sidewalks are full with people soaking up the springtime, the breeze swinging through my window. I am no longer panicked, just unhappy, my hair a mess. I try to knot it in a pony, but realize tying up hair one-handed is no easy task. I try to throw up my hair and catch it; try propping up my head against my bathroom wall. I give up and run a brush through it, toss it to one side.

I think of Nick, his palm against the small of my back. If he was here, he would hook my bra, which is very hard to do without the use of a left arm. I manage, twisting my body, twisting the bra. I think of the way we feed each other oysters, my legs on his legs on tall barstools. He would be cool and collected and know what to do. He would make me smile and then laugh.

Outside, the air feels good on my skin. I feel strong. I get a cab to the hospital.

But Nick is at a party in Brooklyn. Nick is at a party in Brooklyn with his wife.

I text him: *Maybe broke my arm. Heading to St Luke's.*

He calls and says all the right things. "I will come, let me know if you need me. You will be okay. I love you. I'm with you. Keep me updated."

But he isn't with me. He is in Brooklyn at a party with his wife.

And so I update him as the night unfolds so slowly in the fluorescent light of the ER. I flip through my book, and then another, the words unfocused as they make their way to my eyes.

I text: *Saw the triage nurse. Healthy blood pressure! At least.*

I text: *Waiting waiting waiting.*

I text: *A million x rays. Waiting waitinggg tired :(*

He texts back: *You okay? Hang in there. I love you. Text me when you get some info. Don't forget!!!*

He calls, too. He says, "I don't think I can make it there tonight. I want to but I just can't. I'm so sorry. Please understand. I'll come in the morning and take care of you."

And I do understand. It is 2 AM and someone is moaning in a deeper waiting room chamber or in an operating room, if I listen hard. I cry in the metal chair, my arm propped beside me like a broken bird. I feel suddenly deeply tired, tired beneath my bones.

He stops texting and I go home with a sling and a diagnosis: radial head fracture of the elbow. I sleep with my arm on a pillow, my head feeling that empty feeling when you are out of tears.

In the morning, he brings coffee and the paper. He finishes cleaning the floor. He kisses the caved-in joint and my eyelids, and plays me a song on his guitar's smooth belly, and then he has to go. Always he has to go.

I've broken up with Nick, again, this time resolute. I deliver an ultimatum.

"Figure things out with Elena. I can't talk to you unless you are separated."

Nick doesn't want to hear it, argues and argues until his argument loops back again, circles around itself. He loves me, and I don't doubt it.

My love for him feels like a noose. This time, I am firm. I mean it. *Don't date married men* seems more and more like a sound rule. There is no choice but to break my own heart.

"Nick. I love you. If you love me, at least please try to understand."

He says he does. He sings me one of his songs. We hug for hours, and then he leaves. I lock my door behind him. The nights last weeks without him. In the mornings at work, I find notes on my desk: *I respect you. I love you. I'm working on it.* Bottles of Diet Coke, notebooks because he knows I love notebooks, a bracelet. Smiley faces. Emails with audio files of the new songs he's writing for us. I put in my headphones. Every time, hot tears fill my eyes.

I check in with Faith every day. I tell her what I am grateful for: my apartment, spring is coming, I get paid to write about artichokes, my new friends in recovery who understand. I tell her what I'm eating or what I ate. This time, I tell her honestly. When I eat oatmeal, I email her "oatmeal." No longer a secret, the food very slowly loses its tight grip on me. The shame begins to dissipate.

I cry to Faith about Nick, too. It's Saturday morning and I know he must be with Elena. On 95th Street, it seems everyone is coupled, arms around arms, hand in hand. I call Faith.

"I'm so sad," I tell her. "I miss him."

"This self-pity isn't doing you any favors. Where are you?"

"In my neighborhood."

"Want to get a manicure?"

She picks me up in her car and we drive to Long Island, where she's from and manicures are really cheap. I choose orange. On the way home, we stop for iced coffee.

"Hannah." She talks fast. I know she speaks from love. "As we recover, we change. We learn to respect ourselves. We learn to live with integrity. I used to date the most awful men."

"Like Nick?"

"Oh, I've had my share of Nicks."

"So how do you stop the Nicks?" I think of Corey, Ari, Josh. Something is different with Nick. He has gotten way under my skin. Just thinking of him makes my heart feel mangled.

"Time. Recovery. Kindness. Honesty."

She makes it sound so simple.

"I know he's a mess. But he really loves me."

"Oh, girl." Faith takes a long sip of her iced coffee. "Men are going to love you. People are going to love you. Do you know why?"

"I have no idea."

"Because you are lovable. You might not know that yet, but the sooner you know it, the better."

"I don't feel particularly lovable."

"Trust me," she says. "You are plenty lovable. The trick is finding the person you want to love back."

Back at work on Monday, I get an email from Nick: *You have to meet me at our diner.*

Nick—I told you, I can't.

I have news. Big news. Trust me.

When I get there, there is coffee waiting for me, the saucer on top to keep it warm. Nick's smile could kill me dead. Close to him, the little hairs stand up on my arms.

"H Maximus. There are no words for how much I miss you. Living without you is not living."

"I know. Trust me, I know. But you said you understood. You said you'd wait until you worked out your separation."

Nick reaches under the table and unzips his backpack. He pulls out a fat stack of papers.

"I signed this morning. She signed. The mediator signed. We're separated. It's official. Totally, legally official."

"Oh my god."

"Max, I did it."

It feels enormous, the weight of these papers, his electric smile.

"I got a room at the Beacon for a week. Stay with me tonight?"

I reach for his hand across the table. I realize now that I didn't think he would really, actually get separated. It was a cliché I took to heart—a married man won't leave his wife for you. He's done just that. His foot shakes somewhere under our hands.

"I can't believe it."

"I can't believe it, either."

"Are you okay? This is such a big deal. It must be really hard."

"Hannah, not being with you is the hardest thing I have ever done."

The pressure is crushing. My heart is full and happy and stunned.

Cake

At the Beacon, Nick shows me the supplies he has stocked: strawberries and clementines, oatmeal and veggie chips. The hotel room has a little kitchen. There's a window with a view down Broadway, the Empire State Building climbing toward the sky. The bed is dressed in snow white. It's like a tiny, perverse home.

He unpacks his clothes, T-shirts in neat bundles.

"Elena has been packing my bags for thirteen years," he says, his words thick with sadness or something else. I think, *I'm never going to pack your bags for you.*

He puts his hands on my hips. It is a simple gesture but I feel contained here, present in his grip. We make love, him behind me. He is looking at me, and I am looking out the window, the city spread before us.

"We're in the best city in the world, and I'm with the most beautiful girl in the world."

I feel as if we are in another universe altogether.

We have turkey burgers delivered, sweet potato fries. Under the white sheets, we have sex again, and I curl up in him, feel his heartbeat fill the room. In this little nook, I feel our magic, the stratospheric swirl of it. As sure as anything.

In the middle of the night I wake up, damp with panic. He is up, too, the TV lighting up the room in fits and starts, drones and blinks.

"Are you okay?" I ask him. His eyes are wet.

"Hannus Maximus." He reaches for both of my hands. "I'm happy you're here. I can't believe I met you, just a girl in Steve's office."

"I'm not just a girl in Steve's office."

"You're certainly not anymore."

His phone keeps lighting up with messages from Elena. In the big bed, I press my feet against his strong calves.

All week, we sleep at the hotel. He brings the staff pizza from Big Nick's, milkshakes. But we can't live at the Beacon Hotel forever.

"We can stay at my place for a while." His guitar is there, his comfy shorts, a set of gym clothes. My cabinets are full of good olive oil and vinegar.

"That wouldn't be fair to you."

He's right. My place is a studio, and Nick takes up vast space. And plus, Elena is not supposed to know that we are together.

For the next few months, Nick and I embark on a tour of the city. He rents an Airbnb in Harlem, a narrow, dark apartment full of pictures of a smiling couple. We camp there for two weeks, popping their microwave popcorn in their microwave, watching rom coms on their TV, making love and shallow dents on their low foam sofa.

Nick's friend Sam is traveling for work for nearly a month, so next we head to his spot on Avenue B. It's majestically big, with bamboo growing on the patio above matching lounge chairs. We buy handfuls of magazines and read them outside, Pearl Jam on the little radio, perched under the bamboo, which shoots up and up. Sam has a washer and dryer in the apartment, a huge luxury. I wash our pillowcases and sheets and make the bed with everything still warm and dive in. Nick is watering the bamboo, which he does religiously.

Sometimes I go with Nick to the little AA meeting on 98th Street in the room under the church that smells of soup. The place is small and crowded; we're lucky if we get seats. If not, we perch on the window-sill. At first, I feel like a fraud. I am not an alcoholic. But I also feel at home. There are young people and old people in shiny shoes and scuffed shoes and an energy that feels both calm and electric. The stories are alternately sad enough to make me cry and uplifting enough to make me cry. People nod knowingly at everything, laugh easily, trade hugs.

Between AA meetings, there are bottles of red wine and cases of beer and little plastic baggies of cocaine. There are days without these things, too, which Nick tallies fastidiously against the drunk days. He tells me, walking down Broadway, his arm around my shoulder, "You know, it's been five days." Or "I haven't had a drink in a week." I learn that these pronouncements mean he is preparing his next binge.

I know this is bad news and he is bad news. I know I should cut and run. I know better. And yet, here I am.

Sometimes there is weed, too. I love the warm smell. I don't love smoking pot, the way it makes me fuzzy and my head weigh a hundred pounds, but I appreciate the permission it gives me to eat. The munch-ies are socially sanctioned. High, Nick and I devour a whole carton of chocolate mint chip from Il Laboratorio del Gelato. "It's going to melt, anyway," we reason. "Better to eat it first." We drink the melted gelato at the bottom, gelato soup. Summer is coming.

We wander Sam's neighborhood at night, stopping for tacos and tapas and singing in the East Village streets. Nick buys us fancy French soap that smells like the French candies we sell at work in oval tins. We walk into a boutique that carries only arty, pricey hoodies. I slip a hoody dress over my arm to try on. Nick follows me into the dressing room, slips his fingers into my panties as I wiggle out of the dress I'm already wearing.

"Nick, what are you doing?"

"You're wet."

"Nick!"

"Shhh!"

I come standing up in the shop's dressing room, my dress still half over my head, Nick's other hand over my mouth. With Nick, everything is an adventure.

"Is everything okay?" the clerk asks.

"Great," we giggle. Nick buys me the dress.

Nick is going to visit his friend in California for a week. "Max, you can stay at Sam's place if you want. But will you do him a favor and water the bamboo?"

"Sure."

"Sam really loves the bamboo." We're at some suburban Fairway, hanging up signs about grapeseed oil. "He's been so nice to let us stay. The least we can do is take care of his bamboo."

"I got the bamboo covered." The next day Nick takes off for San Francisco and I'm busy at work. Before work, I go to the gym. After work, I head to recovery meetings. After the meetings, I stop by Sam's, fill up his watering can, and douse the tall stalks of bamboo. It's a hot summer and each time I return the ground is parched. I water religiously.

"You could have one of those jobs, for people who get paid to be beautiful," Nick says. He's back in New York and we're horizontal on Sam's couch.

"Like a model? I'm not skinny enough."

"Yes you are."

"Not at all."

"Then like a hostess."

"I've done that! It was hell."

"I love you, Maximus."

I love him so much it aches.

As a thank you to Sam for letting us stay, we fill the kitchen with goodies from Fairway, peanut butter–filled pretzels and blood orange juice, Gouda and prosciutto di Parma. Sam is going away for work, so we can stay there again. But first he is home for a week, and so Nick books another stay at the Beacon Hotel.

I miss my apartment, where I haven't slept in a while or even visited, so we make plans to spend the night there. My favorite Starbucks barista asks me where I've been. Traveling, I tell her.

Back home and perched on my bed, Nick gets us tickets to see Cake in Williamsburg. He loves Cake. I like Cake, too, and I wonder if we will dance the way we do at my place, arms and legs kicking everywhere.

We ride the subway to Williamsburg. Outside the venue, they pat us down. Inside, we get beers, talk to some Russian tourists about Cake, look at each other sideways when we're over chatting with the Russian tourists.

We stake out some territory on the concrete. The place is stark— just pavement and fence, but the air is gentle and Manhattan waves like a flag across the East River. We kiss. Nick's lips are cold with beer. And then he pulls away.

"Hi!" Someone is walking our way.

"Matt!" Nick bear hugs a man in shorts, flip-flops.

"This is Hannah. We work together." Matt gives me a hug, too.

Matt has some kind of hookup, so we leave our little patch of concrete and head to the fenced-off VIP section right next to the stage. When Matt leaves to get us fresh beers, Nick leans in close.

"I'm sorry. Matt knows Elena. So you're just Hannah from work, okay?"

I hate this. The beer is sour in my stomach.

"Fine. Okay."

"Maximus, I'm sorry. It is what it is."

What is it? Nick drinks a lot of beers, fast, and we don't hold hands or stand with our hips touching or kiss. Still, we dance, and Nick wraps his arms around my waist during a slow song. I could fall and fall into his smile. The Russian tourists give us a thumbs up from the other side of the fence. I thumb up back.

Then suddenly, Nick is gone, and it is me and the hot energy from endless bodies pressed against each other and up into the sky, hundreds of mouths wailing.

The wanting courses through me. The bass thrums. Nick is nowhere to be found. I see Matt with two women who have endless skinny legs. People throw their empty cups on the ground. I kick one that's not quite empty, and warm beer rushes up my sandals and between my toes.

The crowd pulsates and cheers. Songs end and begin again. Where is Nick?

I feel his hand on my shoulder.

"Let's get out of here." The show is not even almost over, but I can hear that he is serious.

He weaves through the crowd, fast, pushing his way past when people are slow to step aside. I try to keep up with him. He is nearly running.

When he gets onto Kent Avenue, Nick starts barreling forward, breaks into a full-throttle run.

"What's going on?" I call after him. Is there some emergency? Nick is fast and I can't match his long strides. I play back the course of the night in my head, thinking of what could have gone wrong. I'm pretty sure I've lost him. I slow to a walk. It's a lovely night and Williamsburg is wild with the energy of its hipness, of Friday. People spill out onto the street from bars, eat thick burgers on the sidewalk. I don't know what went wrong. I hate myself for not knowing and Nick for not telling me.

Then there he is on Bedford Avenue, outside the subway station, pacing. He won't look at me or talk to me. His eyes are savage.

"What happened? Are you okay?"

He descends into the subway, his T-shirt disappearing into the crowd. I think about whether to follow him. I could walk around, try on sunglasses, buy myself a fancy sandwich. Instead I step down into the Bedford stop. He is here and not here. I touch his arm by the tattoo on his left bicep.

"Baby. What's going on?"

The crowd is like a fashion show parading before us. He shakes off my hand in one angry shake. We don't speak. When the train comes, I find a seat but he doesn't sit next to me. He stands, arms crossed, shaking. We ride back to my place in silence.

At home in my apartment, all his words come out. His anger sears. His eyes are wet and rimmed in red.

"You whore."

Apparently I was flirting with Matt. Apparently I was flirting with the Russians. Apparently I was flirting with everyone. The absurdity strikes me. If only Nick could crawl into my brain for a moment, he would see clear as crystal that he is the sole object of my everything: longing, infatuation, love, contempt. He is it and there is nobody else. Even less than nobody else. But he is not in my brain, he is high as a rocket ship, his nose running, talking fast, shouting. He takes up so much room in my little apartment that there is no air left for me. I feel myself gasping and shrinking.

Part of me wants to laugh, but my face is wet with tears. Why am I wasting my time, my heart on this? I try to rationalize why Nick is breathing licks of fire, why he thinks I am a whore. Maybe there is some reason that makes this night slightly less horrible.

But I know this is not okay. I do not question my knowing.

"Nick." I interrupt my own crying. "You have to go."

He is pacing, pacing, accruing bigger furor with each step. He's not going anywhere.

"Please go."

My sadness turns into fear. Nick's eyes look inhuman. His body vibrates with rage.

He punches a pillow. Then he punches a wall. I have never seen anyone punch a wall before. It sounds hollow, like he is punching a great abyss. Like he is punching nothing. He lets out an injured dog yowl.

I think, *I have to get out of here.*

I think, *I'll go to Urs's place.* I'll take a walk, at least. I grab keys, wallet, phone, make a break for it.

But Nick presses his body up against my door, blocking my way out.

His hand is red and ragged. I can nearly see it throb.

"I'm sorry. I'm sorry sorry sorry." He bellows so loud I'm sure the neighbors hear us. I'm sure Urs hears us at her place, twenty blocks away.

"Sorry is not enough," I tell him, but he is not listening to me.

He is crying, too, now, in giant sobs. We are crying together. We fall asleep crying, my head on his belly.

The next morning, he whimpers, he is pathetic, hungover, 250 pounds of sorry. My eyes are puffy and I am sorry, too, about everything, but mostly that he is here. I nearly choke on my own anger, sadness, humiliation. *How did I become the kind of girl who falls in love with a man who punches a wall? Who calls me a whore?*

"I can't be with you anymore," I say for what feels like the millionth time. My words barely make it out of my mouth. But when he goes, I tell the doormen, "Please don't let Nick in anymore."

They ask, "Are you okay?"

I tell them I will be.

That night, Nick calls and calls and calls. He texts novels. I don't respond, which doesn't seem to stop him:

> *Maximus, I love you more than I ever thought love was possible. You are the love of my life. I understand. I'm going to get sober. I'm going to a meeting today. I'm not doing it for you but I am doing it for us. You gotta believe in me. Please don't run away.*

How can you be so heartless and ruthless and cruel?

I need you.

*What we have just doesn't exist. I'm not going to find it again.
You're not going to find it again.*

Am I still invited to Passover?

Maximus. Fuck you. You don't do this to someone you love.

I turn off my phone. I walk up and down Broadway. I get a manicure and then bite my nails anyway, chewing my cuticles until they
bleed. I miss him already but I remind myself of the wall. Next to my
closet by the doorway, there is only the faintest scar. But I am made of
softer stuff.

Nick and I haven't spoken in weeks when I get an email with an
attachment. I know I shouldn't read his emails, but I can't stop myself.

I open the attachment.

It is a picture of his ankle. It is a picture of his ankle with a tattoo
on it. *Maximus*, it says, in black ink. His nickname for me. The skin
around it is pinkish, speckled with little ankle hairs. I wonder if it is a
joke but know it is not a joke. I delete the email.

Nick is in my marrow and in my heart, still, but I am on his ankle
in thick black ink. He sees me when he ties his shoes. I step with him
up and down stairs, everywhere he goes.

Nick is doing a good job of avoiding me, working in the stores and
staying away from my office in HQ. I am grateful and also on edge. I
play the songs we wrote together on repeat. It's like bathing in a salty
ocean of sadness. I can't think of what else to do.

Sometimes I have altercations with the food in the office. There is so much of it we have to bring in extra shelves. There is no room for conferencing on the conference table because it is full of boxes of toffee, designer granola and flax crackers, barbecue sauces and chickpea chips.

Our office is the home of the specialty department, which is why we get all of the condiments and antipasti, imports from far-flung places. Hibiscus tea and English cookies called biscuits in crinkly sleeves. Mints spiked with lavender and sea salt caramels. Lentils pink as a sunrise. Hazelnuts covered in chocolate. Whole legs of jamón serrano and wheels of Tête de Moine, a nutty Swiss cheese named after the bald spot on a monk's head.

When I go downstairs to the bakery office or the frozen office, there are babkas and anadama bread, black-and-white cookies and key lime pie, sorbets and frozen yogurt pops and cartons of ice cream. In the deli guy's wing, little plastic containers of egg salad and whitefish salad and slivers of smoked salmon and roast beef cover all surfaces, a perpetual buffet.

I eat all of these things. Everyone who makes food wants to sell it on the shelves of Fairway, and so we receive an endless supply of samples, which are sometimes delicious and sometimes disgusting. I try cocktail-flavored water and protein bars full of crickets. I swallow tomato and olive oil pills, which are supposed to make my skin glow.

There are official tastings once or twice a week, when we're considering a new private label supplier for tomato sauce or chicken thighs and need to make an educated decision. We spoon out bowls of crimson A, B, C, D, and E. B is too sweet. A is maybe too sweet. B and C are too gloopy. The room is split between A and D. And so it goes.

I have a good palate, maybe from all those wine tastings and staff meetings. I am usually invited and always ladylike, even when we're tasting croissants. I take small bites and prolific notes: stunning layers, perfect shattering outside, the dough could be butterier, feels a little dry.

The head baker holds up a piece of croissant innards up to the light, squishes it between her fingers. "Exactly," she says.

Beneath Steve's desk is a big box. Maybe if you were moving, you would use it for linens. But we're not moving, and it is the chocolate box. Not even the chocolate box, just the chocolate *bar* box. Bonbons and other chocolate-covered things decorate his desk, our shelves. The box is full of enough chocolate bars to stock a small shop. Inside are all of the kinds I can think of and plenty I cannot think of—single origin and white chocolate flecked with matcha and banana. Milk chocolate made with water buffalo milk. Sixty-eight and seventy-two and eighty-five percent dark. Ninety-nine percent, even.

What a place for a girl with an eating disorder.

"Here's the stash," Steve says one day, kicking the box out from its hiding place under his desk. "Help yourself when you need a chocolate fix."

University of Pennsylvania psychologist Paul Rozin and French sociologist Claude Fischler conducted a study of food cultures. When French people were asked to free associate after hearing the phrase "chocolate cake," the most common response was "celebration." And for Americans? "Guilt."

Maybe if I grew up French, I would be spared this thing? But I meet French girls with eating disorders, too. They are sharp, funny, and just as fucked up as I am. Nobody is safe.

When my coworkers are around, the box of vice and torture stays quiet. But when the chocolate and I are left alone, anything is possible. If I am lucky, I walk away unscathed. Or manage to break off a piece of 72 percent dark Tanzania with cocoa nibs and feel its warm chocolatiness dissolve in my mouth, which becomes a new mouth, a chocolate mouth, and leave it at that.

Other days, it is a different story. It is war. I start with a shard of peanut butter chocolate, a flavor combination that is proof of humanity's brilliance. That peanut butter chocolate knocks me to the floor. The only possible way to get back up again is with the stunning hot sweetness of white chocolate, a sweetness that floods my brain and body in a whoosh so intense that I need something less sweet to recover. Perhaps some pure 100 percent dark chocolate from Saint Lucia, so bad and bitter it begs for more of that peanut butter chocolate. I could play this miserable game for hours, but the fear that someone working late may see me, the scalding shame that I cannot control myself brings me to pack up my stuff, throw on my jacket, head out onto 125th Street up past the Cotton Club and onto the platform of the subway. Harlem opens its arms, indifferent. No dinner tonight. Maybe I can drag myself to a recovery meeting, where someone will listen and say "Me too." Maybe I will call Faith from my bed, leave a long message on her voice mail, read until my eyes get heavy.

I leave work one day, after a busy day. No chocolate.

"Hannah?" says a blonde lady. She is standing on the street right outside of Fairway HQ. She leans against a big SUV. The wind plays with her hair. She is wearing a quilted jacket, cinched at the waist. I recognize her from the pictures on Nick's phone that I've swiped by again and again—Elena and Nick with a koala in Australia, Elena and Nick in sneakers and windbreakers. It's Elena.

What is she doing here? Does she want to see Nick? But she is looking straight at me, through me. *Shit*, I think, *shit*.

"Hannah? I'm Elena." She's not here for Nick. She's here for me.

"I know you are." How could I not know? Elena has haunted my dreams and here she is, waiting for me in the flesh. She is prettier in person than in the pictures. She looks like a wife. She looks like someone Nick might love. As surprised as I am by her presence, her appearance feels inevitable, too. I have been waiting for this since I kissed Nick in the hardware store two years ago. For a few beats she holds me in a grip with her presence. She glowers. We are silent.

Then Elena opens her mouth and a flood of anger comes out. I can't see her eyes beneath her sunglasses, but I imagine they are stormy.

"I've been wanting to say this to you for months, you bitch. How could you be with someone else's husband? How can you be so stupid? Why don't you mess with men your own age? Do you know what you've done? The hurt that you've caused?"

I've wanted to apologize to her. Now is my chance.

"I'm so, so sorry."

"When I was your age I was reckless and stupid, too. I made my share of mistakes. But I knew better than to intrude on someone's marriage. You fucked up everything."

"I don't have an excuse. I'm sorry."

"Sorry? Do you know what you've done? Of course you don't. Whole families you've ruined. Sorry?" Her words speed up, an efflux so furious it's hard to keep up. She calls me *homewrecker* and *whore*, *clueless* and *fucked up*. *Whore* again. I remember that Nick called me a whore, too. For a while, I just stand there and take it. I can see my coworkers leaving work for the day, closing briefcases in trunks. Elena's presence feels both surreal and totally normal, inescapable.

After a while my ears fill only with the whoosh of wind. Elena's tirade slows. "Elena." Her name is heavy in my mouth. "If you want to talk, I can listen. But I'm not going to stand here while you yell at me."

"I'll yell at you all I want."

"Then I'm going to go." I have to escape. I turn toward Broadway, toward the subway.

"Wait." Her voice is different. She looks calmer. "We can talk."

"I haven't seen Nick in a month," I tell her. It's the truth. I haven't caved since the Cake concert.

"You have no idea how difficult it is, being married to him. He disappears for days. He is the most wonderful person and the most difficult person. Sometimes worse than difficult."

"I know. That's why we're not talking."

"All the drinking and the drugs and the lying. I've forgiven him over and over again."

"I don't know how you did that." I think, *This lady is a saint.* I think, *Why did she do it?* She is alluring, so blonde, thin, an attorney. *Why Nick?* I think of the Cake concert.

"I did everything for him for my whole adult life. I loved him. He was a fuckup and I stood by him. I was loyal. I don't know how he could betray me."

"I don't know, either. As absurd as it sounds, I know he never wanted to hurt you."

"I deserve better." She is almost crying.

"You absolutely deserve better."

We both do, I want to say.

"You two deserve each other."

"I told you, we're not talking."

"Well, you should talk to him. He wants to be with you enough to destroy everything we built."

"I'm sorry. I can't say how sorry I am."

"Maybe it's all for a reason. Anyway. Don't let me stop you. Nick loves you. I hope you know that. You two should be together."

She climbs back into her big car, slams the door behind her, drives off down 125th Street. I stand there for a while, paralyzed. I can't catch my breath.

I call Nick and he answers. "I talked to Elena."

"Why?"

"She came to the office to talk to me."

"Oh my god. Are you okay?"

People are asking me if I'm okay a lot lately. I don't know how to tell. "Can we meet at the diner?"

When I get to the diner, Nick is already at a booth. I tell Nick that Elena gave me, gave us, her blessing.

"I'm sorry you had to go through that," Nick says, but I'm not sorry.

I crawl into the booth beside him. His arm around my shoulder. Again, climactic shifts in the space near him, as if we've entered a different universe. If I was waiting for a sign, here it is: Elena. The fucking stratosphere, compressing. Everything seems to be conspiring for me to be here, right here, next to him. It is taking every ounce of will I have not to see Nick, and it is too exhausting. I am drained. I cannot fight against my own heart anymore. Somehow, despite everything, I love him.

"Don't leave me again. I'm serious."

"Don't worry. I can't."

I mean it. Leaving Nick seems impossible. I've done it so many times, to no avail. I can't imagine having enough energy to leave him again. I can't imagine what I would have to do to make it stick.

Yet when Nick and I are together, I am both exhilarated and plotting my escape. I know dating him is not a sane, recovered thing to do, and yet I cannot pry myself from the way I am with him, the atmospheric bubble we blow. I feel responsible for him, like our love is some kind of pact that necessitates endless coffees at the diner. We can't seem to stay broken up.

Food is a drug I am learning to put down. I reroute the contours of my life without bingeing and starving. Nick is a drug I fiend for still. I hate myself for it. After what seems like forever at the diner we get fro-yos to take back to my apartment, and he sticks them in the freezer and wraps me in a hug so that our whole bodies are not just touching but without boundaries, his skin is my skin, his tattoo is my tattoo, and it is better than chocolate and cake and sex and success and all of the things that are good. How could I possibly do without this?

"I'm sorry it's been like this, Max," he says. He sits on my bed and takes off his shoes and socks, shows me his tattoo. His skin has healed. It looks like it has been there forever.

The next day at work, Bill the CEO calls me into his office. "Are you all right?" Everyone else asks, too. Turns out, they listened to the whole conversation with Elena through open windows.

"I was going to tell her to go away," Bill says. "But you seemed to handle it so well. If she comes back, I can ask her to leave."

"I don't think she'll come back."

On Saturday, Nick and I ride the subway downtown to SoHo together. Nick is going to his friend's son's birthday party. The son is one. I am not going because Elena will be there. Obviously Elena and I cannot both attend a child's birthday party for Nick's friend who is also Elena's friend. The whole situation reminds me again how thorny and mangled everything is, how not right. Nick and I kiss a block away, part ways. I peruse jumpsuits and fedoras that cost more than anything I own. I buy a coffee and read my book and wait.

Nick doesn't take too long at the party. After, he tastes like buttercream frosting.

We hold hands and walk down Spring Street. There is a real estate office with a chalkboard outside: *SoHo open houses today!*

Nick snaps up the first one we see, on Broome and West Broadway, above a swanky glasses shop. It's a one-bedroom walkup, the bedroom is so small it just barely holds a mattress. The four walls do not create a square, more a trapezoid. All of the walls in his new pad are slanty, at irregular angles, so furniture doesn't quite fit. It gives the place a sort of funhouse feel.

I help him move in a U-Haul, lugging stuff up the stairs to the second floor. There is not too much stuff; the whole move takes only a few hours.

We put a futon in the kitchen. There is nowhere else for it to go. It's weird, but it works. Nick scrambles eggs while I read.

Nick needs a mattress, and we go to Sleepy's and lie on everything in the store until we settle on the perfect firm-to-cushy ratio. Delivery will take forty-eight hours, and we need somewhere to sleep tonight.

"We can stay at my place," I suggest.

"We can carry it," Nick says. Fourteenth Street to SoHo. It's not that far.

"Are you sure?" the mattress people ask, but they wrap it in plastic and tie rope handles for us to hold onto.

Outside, the wind slaps around the mattress, slaps us around, too. Nick walks in front so he can navigate past tourists and kids and businesspeople with briefcases. I struggle to get a grip on the thing.

"Can we take a break and readjust?"

We're only at 11th Street and it feels as if we've been trekking for miles. The wind hisses in my ears. I didn't know we were going to carry a mattress today. I didn't wear the right shoes, and my toes squish and throb in my chunky heels under the extra weight.

"I don't think this is going to work."

"Of course it's not going to work if you're not helping."

"I am helping."

"Sure you are."

We flip the mattress the long way instead. Then we flip it back. Then we switch positions, so Nick is in the back. By the time we get to SoHo, we're not talking to each other. We make it up the narrow stairwell, somehow, and collapse on its haunch. The mattress is cold from its journey. Nick doesn't apologize.

I pick a cool sage to paint Nick's bedroom. It's the color of his eyes at dusk. We tape up the moldings, take turns brushing the wall in colorful strokes. I climb up the ladder to get close to the intersection of wall and ceiling. Nick passes the paintbrush up to me. I lean forward to reach the corner when the ladder topples beneath my weight. We haven't locked it open properly, and it folds up in a quick crash. I land on my ass. For a week, the back of my legs are dappled in blue, black, green. Nick takes a bunch of pictures of them, impressed by the artistry of my bruises.

I sit cross-legged on the floor, counting the eighty-four beams that make up his new Ikea bed frame as he lays them out one at a time. Next to me, there is a green-gray streak on the hardwood floor where I dropped the paintbrush. A baseball game is on the radio, narrated by Nick's favorite announcer. I offer to help but he gives me his credit card to buy us sushi across the street.

"You know," he says over spicy tuna rolls. "You killed Sam's bamboo."

"What? I watered that bamboo so thoroughly. How could I have killed it?"

"Well, Sam came back from his work trip and his bamboo was dead as a doornail." He pops a blob of wasabi in his soy sauce, pokes at it with a single chopstick.

"How could that be?" I took good care of that bamboo.

"It's dead. All dried out. And you know how Sam feels about that bamboo. It's like his child."

"Nick, I don't know what to say. I watered the shit out of the bamboo."

"Shit happens, Max," Nick says. "I'll buy Sam new bamboo."

We finish our sushi but never finish painting Nick's bedroom. The tape stays up on the walls, as if any day now we may complete our project.

We decide the bathroom walls should be a sort of notebook, and we scribble lines of songs and things in Sharpie. We write each other acrostics and cryptic messages by the sink, above the toilet. The bathroom gets humid, and the lines begin to wobble and bleed.

When things are good with Nick, they are unfathomable. I've never made out in so many cabs, steadying myself to keep my head safe from plexiglass. We go all over the city, throwing back oysters at fancy places and wrapping ourselves in parts of each other—legs in legs, fingers in fingers. We ride a historic tugboat to Jersey City, the wind in our faces. Nick sings with his friend's bands, and I drink beer with all the girlfriends, dance with them, our bodies touching. Everything is an adventure, every day unlike the day before. Nick writes an album in love songs, more.

"What are you doing next weekend?" he asks in SoHo. We are both reading on the futon in the kitchen. "I could use some fun. We deserve it." He buys us tickets to the Bahamas. We leave in two days.

In a moment of chagrin, I tell him all my bathing suits don't even sort of fit me.

"Let's go shopping, then."

I am grateful to him. The old lady bra store, once a place of horror, is a godsend. They even have bikinis with underwire, with support, for people like me, and I buy two. I model for Nick. "You look hot," he tells me. I don't quite believe him, but I don't completely discount him, either.

We buy stacks of magazines for the plane ride, hand sanitizer, snack-sized bags of almonds. On the beach, I wear my new bikini. We snorkel and write songs in the sand. Under water, my right breast keeps slipping out of my bikini top. Nick laughs at me and my escaped boob. We ride a boat to a little island with hammocks in the trees and a wild boar who lounges in the sun. We slather sunscreen on each other's backs and still burn. Nick peels the flaking skin off my shoulders.

Nick has been sober for months, the longest time in memory, and when people approach him on the beach, in the hotel lobby, with "Want to party?" he laughs.

"Everyone can see I love drugs. It's as if it's tattooed on my face."

But we say no thank you and buy Ben & Jerry's for five times the price it would be in New York. "I really want to drink," Nick tells me, again and again, but we swim and chug Diet Coke and have sex on a blanket in the sand at night, the sky another blanket above us.

"I'm proud of you," I tell him.

We go to an AA meeting on a dirt road, then browse Bahamian junk food in shiny bags at a stale-aired bodega next door. Inside the brick church where the meeting is held, there are five people who tell stories of drunken nightmares and sober nightmares and waking up, against all odds. The meeting makes me feel like I am doing something important, productive, being here. I think maybe Nick could be a sane, sober person that I wouldn't be embarrassed to bring to dinner with Ursula, to Passover. Anything seems possible.

Back on the beach we see the baseball announcer from the radio. "I'm going to say hi," Nick says, excited, and talks to him for nearly an hour. I watch them over the pages of my book.

After dinner, we walk on the docks by yachts with names like *Black Swan* and *Couples Therapy*. The sun skitters on the water.

"Let's get married," Nick says.

"Nick, you're already married."

"But not for much longer. And not to you."

"Maybe finish this current marriage first."

"Let's have babies one day. And a house by the ocean. You can write books. You can write our story."

I smile and kiss his salty sea lips. My heart burns hot and deadly as the sun. And yet. The thought of a life with Nick is the thought of a roller coaster. I don't even like roller coasters. I think of the drugs and the wall and how we started things, with secrets and lies. And love. I think of Elena. The water caresses the shore. Or is it a smack? A series of small, infinite smacks.

The six-month lease on Nick's SoHo apartment is ending, and he wants to find a place where we can live together soon, where the futon doesn't smell like cooking oil.

I'm at work, writing press releases for our new flash-frozen French macarons when I notice one missed call from Nick, then two. Number three, I pick up.

"Hey babe, sorry, I'm on a deadline for this."

"Hi! Max! I found a killer apartment."

"That's awesome. Can I see it soon? After work?"

"Come see it now!"

"I'd love to, but it's the middle of the day, and it's a little crazy here."

"Max, I wouldn't ask if I didn't mean it. I want to get us this apartment and I want to do it now. It's dreamy. Jump in a cab, on me. You'll be here in a flash and nobody will even notice you're gone." He is a puppy dog, and I don't want to let him down.

"Fine. Text me the address."

There is a river of traffic on the West Side Highway and I curse myself for being so easily persuaded. It's hot. When I roll down the windows, noxious air surges into my mouth, thick with gas. Everything smells like sawdust and motor oil and sweat. By the time I get to midtown, I'm grouchy and impatient.

The apartment building looks like a fancy hotel, and its AC jolts me alert. Nick meets me at the lobby, his smile more radiant than the chandeliers that cast us in twinkly light. He kisses me. "Wait 'til you see this place." He beams.

There's a salesperson, serious in her saleslady suit, stilettos nearly as tall as the building's sixty-three floors behind her. She shakes my hand, clicks her way into the elevator that whisks us up to the apartment.

It's a white box, everything shiny from just being built, innocuous in its expensive perfection. But out the window is an expanse of sky that doesn't end. And below the cotton-ball clouds, the rest of Manhattan, its towers like toy buildings, the grid of streets, the miniature traffic, the blue-gray Hudson, New Jersey. I am floored.

"Check out the kitchen, Max."

It is a pretty sweet kitchen: fancy appliances, drawers that close themselves, an island bigger than my apartment. But the thing about the kitchen is that it looks out over the wide world.

The saleswoman clicks us around the rest of the building. There is a private Equinox gym, a basketball court, a movie screening room, a pool. I think of my studio, the SoHo apartment with the futon jutting out into the kitchen, how you have to turn sideways to squeeze out of bed. This place is absurd.

"Can we have a second?" Nick asks the saleslady.

He grips my hand. "Do you love it?"

"Of course I do. What's not to love? But shouldn't we look at some other apartments first, to be sure? Isn't this insanely expensive? I didn't even know you were looking yet."

"Max, let me do this for us! For you!"

My phone keeps buzzing with emails from work. I'm supposed to be there, at my desk. I have a meeting I'll have to sweat to get back in time for.

"Can you really afford it?" This extravagance does not come cheap. I know Nick has money, but this much money?

"Sure. Listen, I know it's been rough. I want you to have a beautiful kitchen to cook in. I want you to have everything."

"Let's look at some more apartments, just to be safe."

"Why? This one is perfect. Isn't it?"

"It's incredible."

I sit down with Nick and he signs the lease, the building amenities charge, all of the other fees and disclaimers, our knees touching under the table. I get a cab back to work with the new key on my key ring, a fob for the "sky lounge" and the yoga studio. I may or may not be late to my meeting. Nick forgets to pay for the cab and in the excitement, I forget to remind him. To me, cab fare is a significant amount of money.

There are things Nick doesn't like about me. Sometimes, when Steve and I talk about books, Nick accuses me of pretention. He says the way I crunch apples, so loud and percussive, is disgusting. (I make sure to cut up my apples into neat wedges in his presence after that.) I say "like" too much. I sometimes dress too revealingly and other times too sloppily. I hold my purse wrong—he calls it "easy steal," though the only time I've been robbed was at gunpoint. I am too flirty. I am too dependent on my friends. I take my recovery too seriously. I take everything too seriously.

My sponsor Faith dumps me because of Nick.

I have my own issues with codependency, with dating addicts, she writes in a long email. *It's too close to home, it's triggering for me to hear about it. I hope you leave him for good. In the meantime, I don't think I can help you.* I am stunned. I've failed myself, and Nick, and now her, too.

I go to meetings every day I can. My new sponsor Aaron is a Big Book traditionalist. His sponsees, most of us women, meet together for close readings of the Big Book at one of our apartments in Stuy Town. We jokingly call it Bible Study. Aaron went to yeshiva as a kid, and the meticulously close readings remind me of college, the obsessive dissections of text, literary criticism, but we all share our stories. "Bill's story has to become your story," he says, of the blue book originally published in 1939, of its author, the creator of twelve steps. "Or else it's of no use." So we tell each other our darkest secrets, training for marathons only to binge until we were sure we had broken some internal organ, taking laxatives by the fistful. Aaron used to weigh five hundred pounds. Today he looks like a normal guy, fit from martial arts and turkey sandwiches.

It's working, going through the steps in the Big Book. I am changing. I rack up a year without starving myself, bingeing, without hurting myself with food, which seems a bona fide miracle.

"This is not a diet," Aaron says a million times. "It's not the recovery and swimsuit modeling club." It's all about the food but it's not about the food. Which is to say food is but a symptom. Which is to say that when I change my head and my heart, when I take care of myself, when I live with honesty and integrity, I no longer have the furious urge to carve my flesh off my body, to eat whole plates of cookies meant for large parties of hungry people.

Nothing precipitates the final breakup. Or everything does. I'm talking to Aaron on the phone.

"I know I have to leave Nick," I tell him. "But I am terrified. I love him in a way that I have never felt. And our lives are so enmeshed."

"Enmeshed? Do you live together?"

"No." I'm so grateful that I still have my studio on 95th Street.

"Are you married? Engaged?"

"No."

"Are you pregnant?"

"God no."

I see that there are two ways to move forward, with or without Nick. I think about moving in to his fancy new apartment, getting married. I think about years passing with him, decades. The thought makes me want to puke. I think about what I want from my recovered life. Who I want to be and be with—someone I respect and admire. Someone I can trust.

It's nearly Christmas, and I don't want to break up with Nick before Christmas. But after Christmas comes New Year's, and then Nick's birthday in January, Valentine's Day, and suddenly I see there is no way but out and no time but now, this very second.

I decide to tell Nick out and about, in public, or else we may stay in my apartment or his apartment for all of eternity. It is unseasonably warm, windy. I wait for him in the inner circle of Columbus Circle. I can't remember what I say, only that at first he stands there arguing with me, refusing to believe it.

"I got a divorce for you. I got sober for you."

I realize he has done everything and that there is nothing left.

"I'm so sorry. You don't have to do anything else for me."

He turns his back and walks away from me. I watch his fast gait, his wide shoulders, his blond head, and then I watch them disappear. I stay for who knows how long, my scarf blowing in the gust, the traffic encircling me, the wind drying my unending tears.

I know this is the last time.

I know this is the real recovery.

Nick must understand that I mean it this time. He doesn't call or text. He doesn't leave drawings at my desk, gifts with my doormen. He comes to pick up his things, his guitar when I am not home, leaves his key and a note that says, *Max, I believe in you. Never forget.*

I don't want to eat. My stomach is sour, bowling-ball heavy, and loving food feels not so much wrong as absurd, a foreign memory, like kissing the spot above his temple, like his fingers intertwined in mine. Urs buys us a bottle of crémant and we toast to new beginnings, although I'm still drowsy with sadness.

I keep calling my friends, Aaron, my mom, to reassure me that I did the right thing. I know that it can no longer be undone. I am twenty-five, almost twenty-six. I wonder if this is it for me, if the atmosphere is never again going to undulate, capsize, if I will have to live the rest of my life confined by earth.

I know better than to wear makeup. I cry on the subway, I cry in kickboxing class, I cry when writing copy about local seafood for work.

Urs takes us to get massages, and I can't stop crying. The massage guy keeps asking "Too hard?" and I keep saying, through sniffles, "No, perfect." But through the salty veil of my tears, I am more and more clear I made the right decision, the only possible one.

I see Nick four months later, at the New York International Olive Oil Competition in SoHo. "Maximus," he says, and opens his arms for a hug. I might drown in that instant in his arms.

"There's something I need to tell you," he says. "Let's go outside for a second." On Crosby Street, we squint in the sun. It's his old neighborhood, our old neighborhood, and the whole place feels painted with sorrow.

He lifts his hand. On his finger, a gold band.

"I got married."

I am stunned. I am still in love with him. It's been just a season since I woke up to his love songs, his head on my belly, since the Bahamas.

"Are you joking?" He must be joking. Who gets married in such a short period of time?

He is not joking. He tells me she is a customer at Fairway, an opera singer, buys good olive oil, that they have talked for years.

"Now you and I can start all over again," he says, laughing. "If you're still harboring a crush on me."

I smile. I am harboring not so much a crush but a pulverized heart.

"If you're happy, I'm happy," I say, because it seems the right thing to say. We step back into the event, apart. A man presents a PowerPoint. Harsh lighting casts everyone yellowish.

I wonder if someone can actually die from sadness. How could someone get to marry Nick so quickly? And at the same time, I feel a surge of sweet relief. I'm glad it is not me.

I'm early to a recovery meeting and scrolling through Facebook on my phone. I see something weird: *RIP Josh, we love you. We're eating a hamburger for you today.* It must be a weird joke. Then an email pops up. It's from Manny at Casellula:

I just saw the news about Josh. I'm so sorry. I know he was your friend.

Was my friend? Past tense?

I Google around. It's true. Josh went to the James Beard Awards in Chicago, like the Oscars for restaurants. He stayed out all night for karaoke. Typical Josh, never one to miss a party. He drowned in the shower of his hotel and didn't make it to the James Beards the next night. He was forty-seven.

What am I to do? I find a chair in the circle at the meeting. I raise my hand to share. "My friend just died," I tell the group. Jenny passes me a tissue, and the woman next to me puts her hand on my arm. It doesn't feel real. I have so much to tell Josh.

The appropriate way to commemorate Josh's death would be to binge. Greasy Chinese food, pizza, hamburgers of course, something fatty and meaty. But I go for a walk with Jenny. It's high spring in Central Park, everything blossoming, wedding photo shoots, kids playing Frisbee. Back home, the sadness chokes me. I call Tom. I call Aaron. I call my mom. I text Dan.

Instead of eating, I write about Josh. He could be a true mensch and an epic jerk. He had a desperate need to be successful, always more successful than he was; accepted. More than accepted—loved. I understand that need. I read everything that food blogs and papers write about him. I wish he could be here to read these things. The food world is gushing about how important he was, such gigantic personality, so smart, so unafraid to piss people off, so true in his love of meat and good food, his quest for that goodness. I wish he could feel the love now.

There is a thing called the baby elephant principle. Circus trainers will tie a baby elephant to a baby stake in the ground. Baby elephants are cute and relatively little (about two hundred pounds little at birth), so it doesn't take much restraint to keep them in line. The animals try to wiggle and force their way out, to break free, but they're chained to a stake. They are stuck. Eventually, they give up.

The babies grow up into grown-up elephants, weighing in at several tons. A little stake should mean nothing for these powerful creatures. They could break the chains that bind them with a flick of their majestic trunk, a shimmy of their tree-trunk legs. But they stay put. The psychological dynamic is more powerful than physical force. They are trapped not so much by the trainers but by their own minds. They have lost hope.

I am an elephant.

Recovery rewires my brain, very slowly.

I once thought I was eternally fucked.

They tell me "a power greater than myself can restore me to sanity." I say that I don't understand what the fuck that means. I don't know that I've ever felt especially sane.

It means hope.

It means that my future is not necessarily in captivity, like a circus animal.

I hear something that nearly breaks my mind: "Many of us had moral and philosophical convictions galore, but we could not live up to them even though we would have liked to."

I would have liked to. I believed a woman's worth and her body were totally unrelated, except for my own. Every fleshy part of me was proof of my failure. I believed I knew better.

Being wounded isn't wrong. Being wounded is human.

That is my beginning.

I ask myself, *What is the best I can do right now?* I try to be okay with whatever that is. And also, I try to do it. I ask the thumping of my heart, *What do you know to be true?* I try to listen, and then to proceed based on that truth. I know exactly who I am and what I'm doing. I've always known, I just didn't trust myself. On good days, sometimes, I do.

And yet. It's a painstakingly slow process. So slow that today, five years later, I wake up in panic that my belly has ballooned, my waist has disappeared in layers of my own flesh. I still have the fear that if I let go of my unrelenting grip of vigilance and obsession I am going to wake up three hundred, four hundred, five hundred pounds, obliterated in folds of fat.

I try on a pair of jeans from the deepest abyss of my closet and wiggle them up only halfway before seeing it will take more than a wiggle to get them around the expanse of me. I throw them in my trash can in disgust. On my way to work, I toss the trash down the chute. I can't bear the ghost of the thinner me lurking around in my apartment.

I stop for coffee. Spring is flirting with daffodils in planters and buds on trees and the sun is kind on my face.

The twelve steps are about surrender to something that is not me. And so I pray, as my boots take me to work, to something I may or may not believe in, anything at all that may save me from myself.

Please. It is always *Please please please. I am twenty-nine. I don't want to be thirty, forty, fifty and at war with myself, day after day. I don't want every day to be about losing one more pound.*

I have big dreams today. For twenty-five years, my biggest dream was to lose another pound.

I know my eyes are broken because I see the picture from a college party. It is senior year, and so there are more parties than ever. Facebook tells me today is seven years later. Seven years ago, seeing that picture was a hot slap. My arms! They looked fat as the sausages hanging in stout rounds in windows in Little Italy, I was sure. I was sure I looked less like a human girl and more like a bovine. Because of the picture, I forbade myself the indulgent luxury of dinner. Because of that picture, I ran on the elliptical until I ran out of songs on my little green iPod. I swathed myself in my red quilt and read and read and stopped to cry and then to pass out. The next morning, I threw away the dress, the evidence. As if it were the dress's fault.

Seven years later, I look again. My arms are wrapped around Urs, and they look like fine arms to me now, good human arms, not even particularly fat. Our smiles are wide and true. I am sad for my former self, sad that I missed seeing all that love, riding its waves. All I could see were my arms, and, I now realize, I couldn't even see them.

Still, I wake up with that feeling that I am a monster. Even my organs are monster organs, my monster kidneys and monster spleen cry out. My monster body is a betrayal. I try to remember that I felt a monster seven years ago, felt it to be true as anything, and yet I was not a monster, not even close.

I text two people I respect. Two beautiful women who have been where I have been. *OMG I know it's not the truth but it feels as real as anything, that I am so fat today, so not okay, not enough, hideous. It's scary how real it feels.*

One woman says, *I hear you. You are beautiful but you don't have to believe me. Just act as if you are perfect, how you are supposed to be. Pretend. Use it as a working hypothesis. Try it on for size.*

What would my life be like if I believed I was beautiful? This seems like a stretch. So I try, *What would my life be like if I believed I was okay?*

The other woman says, *Get out of yourself and your own head. Call someone else. Ask how they are doing. Ask about their day. Listen. Don't talk about you.* That advice. I've heard it before from Aaron and it is exactly what I don't want to hear. It works nearly every time.

I go to work and I get distracted writing a brochure, doing my job. A coworker is talking about eyelash extensions, and I think about eyelash extensions for a minute, instead of the way my pants choke me, and I feel a little better. I stop to make myself a peppermint tea, and the office manager and I talk about how icy blue the sky is today.

Cotton-ball clouds dot the expanse out the window, all the way to New Jersey.

During lunch, I take a walk. There is a church on Hudson Street with a little garden. I sit on the bench for a minute. It's me and a woman in a giant coat. I am still plenty fucked up, but at least I am not alone with it. Even on the worst days, I hold onto that hope with all of me. I need those worst days to bring me back to the simple fact that I am hurting, I am longing, my heart is open.

Together, we are broken and strong, odd and worthy, emotional and more triumphant than I ever could have guessed.

Recovery takes courage and kindness.

It doesn't happen overnight. But I change.

I start to talk to Ursula. "I'm so sorry I wasn't there for you when you were suffering." She holds me in a hug.

"But you were there." It was me who was somewhere else.

When Urs makes a big buffet of fruit and cheese and chocolate at her new place in Berkeley where she is working to get her doctorate in music composition, cranberry-walnut bread and dried peaches, I still eat a little too much, nibble when my belly says it may be wiser to stop.

But I don't use food as a drug.

I don't use it as a bullwhip.

I don't eat the whole wheel of cheese. I don't say *fuck it*.

And if I do eat the whole wheel of cheese, if I do say *fuck it*, I don't punish myself the next morning, the next week, the next year.

I put life first.

I help others. I mentor a bunch of women who want to recover, too. They call me, crying, from the scale, just as I have people to call, crying from the scale.

I hope that if I have daughters, children, I won't pass on this particular pain. I'm sure they will have their own problems, but I hope they see me licking a cone of gelato with joy. I hope when they look in the mirror they smile.

I notice that the people who love me do not love me more or less if I am thinner or heavier. One morning, I wake up with an angry crimson rash on my face and neck. Worse than the itching is how crazy I look. I am embarrassed to leave my apartment. "You are so much more than your face," Aaron tells me when I call him. *Am I?* Almost certainly, I am more than my face and more than my body and more than the way my thighs rub together under my summer dress.

My eating disorder is all about me, me, me. A selfish beast. It tricks me into thinking that if I can shrink enough, I will be safe and loved and admired. But I am safe and loved and admired just as I am, no matter what size I wear, even if I have to tell myself this a million times over to half believe it.

It makes me sad, how much of my own life I have missed, buried in the self-obsession of my eating disorder. The azeitão wasn't supposed to deliver pain and redemption. It was just cheese. Yes, transportive, historic, symbolic, important, but still just cheese, some delicious fermented milk, no more, no less.

Sharing my story, doing this recovery thing with others, is so much bigger than myself. I reach out for help, every day. Together we get better. I don't have to be alone anymore, unless I want to be. Jenny's new music manager wants her to lose weight and so Jenny dumps the music manager and finds a new one. "I'm so proud of you," I tell her. She is brave.

I too am brave. I miss Nick but I don't call him. I play his love songs until I stop playing them. I know I am ready for a different kind of love. I've been in a healing intensive. My heart has broken and healed and broken and healed. There is a Japanese art called *kintsukuroi.* Each time a piece of pottery cracks, it is lacquered back together with gold. All those golden threads make the piece what it is, extraordinary.

I like to think of my heart like that. That each time it breaks, it gets more valuable and beautiful with the mending. It is a collage of gold.

I think of the trees in a forest, the beautiful trees. Their beauty is not diminished by the way they bend in the wind, creaky, the way one branch is longer than another branch. Maybe there are supermodel trees, too, but I love the squat ones, and the asymmetrical ones, the ones that bow their heads to make a canopy, under which I raise up my arms and open my mouth because the beauty demands nothing less.

On good days, I know my eating disorder is a gift. A burden, an agony, and, still, a gift. Golden. Once I come to know my pain, to see it for what it is, it is mine to glean. The fields of my pain blossom with experience, wisdom. Wildflowers and tangles of growing things. I pick them like grapes from a vine. The grapes are juicy with promise that doesn't run out. I press them into wine. Wine that is fuel. Fuel that turns heartache into an opportunity, inspiration. Everything I'm looking for is here, of course. Where else would it be?

Because at the end of the day, what I'm looking for is worth and faith. I'm hungry for the conviction that my truth is true enough, bright enough, and that who I am is entirely enough. It's a daily struggle for me because I'm an addict, but also because I'm an artist, a writer, a woman, and also because I'm a human being.

It's not that I've emerged from my cocoon a butterfly. It's not that I have escaped the taskmaster that lives in my brain and shouts and shouts an endless loop of fear, worry, shame. But I do know that the taskmaster's voice speaks only some garbled, deeply skewed version of the truth, and that's no truth at all.

I'm less afraid to fall into the depths of my fear, worry, shame. I've been there, and I know the way back out again. I have a flashlight. The darkness cannot devour me, and it certainly cannot stop me. Every bad moment is not a judgment. Every bad decision is not a life sentence.

Dan and his boyfriend Jake are coming to visit from Boston and London—they're still together and still long-distance after all these years. "I'm going to cook you dinner if that's cool," I tell Dan on the phone.

"When have I ever said no to you cooking me dinner?"

At the greenmarket by Lincoln Center, I walk by a table of mushrooms—hens-of-the-woods, chanterelles, oysters. And the prices? Not exorbitant! I buy enough to fill my whole tote bag.

Next I visit my guys at the Fairway cheese counter for a hunk of lemony chèvre and Parmigiano-Reggiano.

"What are you cooking?" And I tell them. They give me a wedge of Stilton for free, just because.

I stop at Barzini's for Honeycrisp apples. I walk home smiling, my arms full.

I call Aaron. "I'm cooking a big dinner. I don't want it to be a big *thing*. I don't want it to lead to a binge."

"That was before," he says. "You're in recovery now. Enjoy the dinner. Enjoy your friends. Text me if you need to."

It sounds so simple. I bake an apple crumble, topped with oats, brown sugar, and walnuts. When Dan and Jake arrive, my apartment smells of butter.

"I'm making mushroom risotto." I hug them one-handed, my spatula in the other. "Tell me everything about Boston and London and life."

They do and I listen. I tell them about Fairway and breaking up with Nick, and Jake slings a long arm around my shoulder. I sauté my mushroom bounty until it turns a deep gold. The risotto comes out creamy and perfect. I serve myself a spoonful, neither gigantic nor tiny.

Dan finishes up the last bites from the pot. "You haven't lost it," he says. "This is too good."

I've lost something else, though. It's late by the time they leave. My playlist repeats from the beginning. I wrap up the apple crumble and put it in my fridge. I don't hate myself for eating real food with butter and sugar and Arborio rice. I don't need to devour every last edible thing in my kitchen, either.

Even when this recovery is painstakingly, teeth-grittingly hard, the magic is here. Right here. There is no butterfly. There is only me.

ACKNOWLEDGMENTS

My heart is full. Thank you to my agent Andrea Somberg for believing in *Feast*, and to its first editor, Morgan Parker, for nursing it into being. Thank you, Laura Van der Veer for adopting this book as your own. You are a fierce editor, and I am lucky to work with you. To the team at Little A, I am grateful for everything you do.

Thank you for your friendship and brilliance, Kate Fridkis Berring, Yelena Schuster, Kelsey Blodget, and Carolyn Kylstra.

Thank you for your generosity in reading and in all things, Rena Mosteirin.

Thank you for being there always, Ursula Kwong-Brown.

Thank you for your wisdom Ben Anastas, Joan Wickersham, and the rest of the incredible community at the Bennington Writing Seminars.

To my mom and dad, Rachel and Marty Howard, there is no way to thank you for your unending love, kindness, and support.

Anthony Mulira, I love you always and with all of me.

ABOUT THE AUTHOR

Photo © 2016 Vlad Kfrg

Hannah Howard is a writer and food expert who spent her formative years in New York eating, drinking, serving, bartending, cooking on a hot line, and flipping giant wheels of cheese in Manhattan landmarks such as Picholine and Fairway Market. She received her BA from Columbia University in creative writing and anthropology in 2009. She is currently pursuing her MFA in creative nonfiction at the Bennington Writing Seminars, where she is a recipient of the Lucy Grealy Scholarship. Her work has been published in *New York* magazine, *VICE,* and *Self.* She also mentors women recovering from eating disorders by helping them build happy, healthy relationships with food and themselves. She lives in New York City.